THE G
COACH GUIDE

England Through the Big Window

Elizabeth Gundrey

CENTURY PUBLISHING

LONDON

First published in Great Britain in 1983
by Century Publishing Co. Ltd
76 Old Compton Street, London W1V 5PA
ISBN 0 7126 0100 7

Photoset in Times by
Rowland Phototypesetting Ltd
Bury St Edmunds, Suffolk
Printed in Great Britain by
Hazell, Watson & Viney
Aylesbury, Bucks

Cover and text design by Jim Wire
Cover illustration by Bill Le Fever

THE GOOD COACH GUIDE

THE AUTHOR

Elizabeth Gundrey has written a number of books about travel in this country – *England by Bus* (Hamlyn), *Staying Off the Beaten Track* (Hamlyn), *England by the Sea* (Severn House) and, to be published later this year, *Elizabeth Gundrey's Pick of Cumbria*. She contributes regularly to the travel pages of the *Observer* and to other newspapers and magazines. Her numerous publications have included books and articles about consumer affairs, and about activities for children.

NOTE

Places to Visit, given at the end of each chapter, are all within a bus-ride of about ½ hour from the coach station. + indicates good sites for picnicking.

The dates given for **Annual Events** are approximate.

Illustrations by kind permission of the following.

Brighton Pavilion *courtesy of Brighton Resort Services Department*; Palace Street and The Cathedral, Canterbury *courtesy of John Berbiers*; The Promenade, Cheltenham *courtesy of Cheltenham & Gloucester Building Society*; Pilot Street, King's Lynn *courtesy of King's Lynn Preservation Trust Limited*; Lowestoft Highlight and Beccles from the River *courtesy of Waveney District Council*; Severns Building, Nottingham *courtesy of City of Nottingham Public Relations Office*; St Michael's Mount near Penzance *courtesy of Penwith District Council*; Peterborough Cathedral from an old print; The Barbican, Plymouth *courtesy of Chris Robinson, New Street, Barbican*; the *Mary Rose*, Portsmouth, from an old print; Salisbury Cathedral, from an old print; The Abbey, Sherborne *courtesy of the Tourist Information Centre*; Bear Steps Hall, Shrewsbury *courtesy of Shrewsbury Civic Society*; The Inner Bailey, Taunton Castle *courtesy of Somerset County Museum Service*; Friar Street, Worcester *courtesy of Worcester City Museum Service*; Abbeydale Industrial Hamlet, Sheffield *courtesy of Publicity Department, City of Sheffield*; Jarrow Hall, Newcastle upon Tyne *courtesy of Northumbria Tourist Board*; The Guildhall, Carlisle *courtesy of City of Carlisle*; The City Museum, Lancaster, drawing by David Oldroyd, from *A Walk around Historic Lancaster* by John Champness; Wool Exchange, Bradford *courtesy of Bradford Economic Development Unit*.

CONTENTS

INTRODUCTION   page 9

What is a coach? The coach network. What coach travel is like. The cost of coach travel. Coach versus car. Activity holidays by coach. Where to stay. When and where to go. What every traveller should know

DAY OR WEEKEND TRIPS

Brighton	23	Peterborough	101
Bury St Edmunds	32	Plymouth	111
Canterbury	40	Portsmouth	120
Cheltenham	53	Salisbury	128
King's Lynn	61	Sherborne	139
Lowestoft	71	Shrewsbury	144
Nottingham	79	Taunton	152
Penzance	92	Worcester	159

A TOUR OF THE NORTH   page 165

Sheffield   167   Newcastle   174   Carlisle   182
Lancaster   188   Bradford   196

APPENDICES

Tourist Boards	204	City Weekend Breaks	206
Where I Stayed	204	Explorer Tickets	206
Hostels	205	Coach Companies	207
Other Scenic Routes	205	Acknowledgements	208

ROUTES DESCRIBED IN THE BOOK

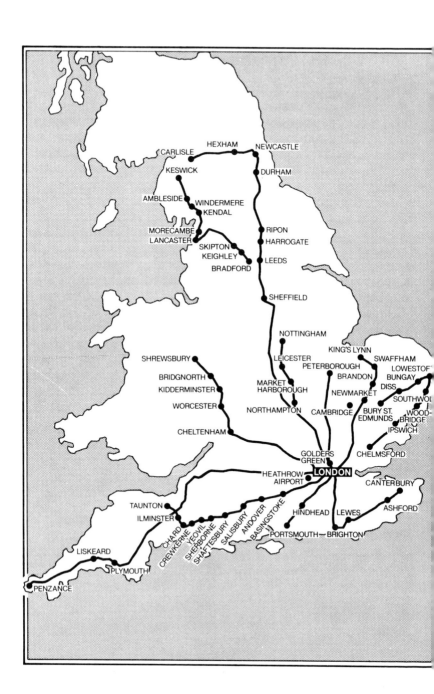

INTRODUCTION

What is a Coach?

In America, they call them buses. But to the British, a bus is the unpretentious vehicle that jogs slowly along, stopping frequently and calling at obscure places to pick up shoppers or schoolchildren. A coach is far more luxurious than this, speeding along the motorways and main roads from one city to another with few stops.

Buses have their charms, and I have written about them at length in *England by Bus*, describing my ramblings along country byways to villages 'unknown to grandeur and unknown to fame'. But it is a way of travel, relaxed and rural, that takes time.

This book about coaches is for those who want to go farther and to go faster. And, because the coaches' destinations are towns or cities, this is a more urban book.

In each chapter, I describe my journey and then places of interest in the immediate vicinity of the spot where the coach set me down (almost invariably, right in the centre of a city or town). So anyone wanting merely to make a day-trip, or (by booking two tickets) to pause for a couple of hours en route to somewhere else, would, with the help of this book, be able to find plenty to see even in such limited time, and without walking far. But for those with a couple of days to spare, there are lists of what can be seen by going a little further afield.

The Coach Network

The only organisation with nationwide coverage is National Express. Its 1,500 white coaches nip along the highways to over 3,000 destinations – carrying people on some 12 million trips every year. There are hundreds of other coach companies, but each of these provides only regional coverage (some one-man firms are very localised indeed): the biggest ones are listed on p. 207.

The frequency of the coaches varies a good deal (usually,

there are more in summer than in winter) so the information in this book should be checked before making plans. The coach station in any town can give you information and book seats for you; about 3,000 travel agents in the country also sell coach tickets and have timetables; or you can telephone any of the following numbers on any day of the week, from 8 a.m. (until 6.30 p.m., unless otherwise stated) for details, and to make bookings (quoting your credit card number is acceptable to most companies provided you book more than a week ahead). Or buy a complete book of all the NE timetables if you want to work out your own itinerary (NE also sell a very large map of their network). For London-based travellers there is 'Sixty Principal Destinations', a free booklet of times and fares. For the disabled, there is a special leaflet about how to travel by coach.

National Express Offices

Birmingham 021 622 4373. Credit Card booking no. 021 622 4225
Bournemouth 0202 21481
Brighton 0273 606600
Bristol 0272 541022
Cambridge 0223 355554
Cardiff 0222 44751
Cheltenham 0242 584111
Exeter 0392 215454
Lincoln 0522 42668
Liverpool 051 709 6481. Credit Card booking no. 051 709 6485

London 01-730 0202 until 10 p.m. Credit Card booking no. 01-730 3499
Manchester 061 228 3881. Credit Card booking no. 061 228 3591
Newcastle 0632 616077
Northampton 0604 24544
Norwich 0603 20491
Nottingham 0602 585317
Peterborough 0733 313159
Sedgfield 0740 22539
Sheffield 0742 754905
Thanet 0843 581333
Wakefield 0924 363166

Although it is easy to find out where National Express coaches go from and to, you need a crystal ball for all the others, because there is no one timetable book or route map with all of them in it. In London, they have a bewildering variety of departure or picking-up points: on p. 167 I describe how I located, only by sheer chance, a quite large coach station hidden in a hotel basement! It is easier for a spy to penetrate national security than for would-be passengers to unravel the mysterious movements of the coach industry.

National Express operates a carefully planned interchange system at several key cities into which coaches pour from all over the country: London, Cheltenham, Sheffield, Bristol, Exeter and Birmingham. So changing from one coach route to another is simple – no cross-city journeys or stairs between one coach and the next. The coaches are timed to allow ample changeover time – though, inevitably, there are occasional breakdowns of the system. If one incoming coach is badly behind schedule, several others may have to await it before departing.

What Coach Travel is Like

Most coaches seat 50 people – in rather more comfort than on airplanes, for example. Being a six-footer, I make for the seats behind the driver or next to the emergency door because these have most leg-room – but the others aren't bad as a rule (though some companies do put in more seats at the expense of leg-room) and I have rarely travelled on a coach where I did not have a double seat to myself, although this is less likely at weekends. The driver's side is also the one to make for when travelling north if you don't want to be exposed to the afternoon sun. But the other side is the one with traffic-free views.

Seats are comfortable, with headrests, overhead lights and adjustable ventilators; and coaches are clean. (At least, most coaches are like this – some operators have lower standards.) A few coaches have tinted windows or else blinds to use when the sun streams in; and in some the angle of seat-backs is adjustable. Windows are huge, so – coaches being much taller than cars – one gets excellent views, over walls and hedges, and into people's gardens. Because coaches (unlike most trains) go through town centres, the scene is more varied, occasionally with close-ups of cathedrals or castles, for instance. The ride is usually very smooth, but this depends more on the roads than the coaches. Smokers are confined to the rear seats.

Although there are racks for hand-luggage, it is a distinct advantage that big suitcases are lifted in and out of the boot by the driver: a touch of personal service rare these days. Most drivers are very helpful to elderly people, children travelling alone or disabled people: I encountered only one grouchy one.

On longer journeys, refreshment stops of ¼ to ¾ hour are allowed for in the timetable – a welcome break for eating, w.c., nappy-changing or just a stroll to stretch one's legs (though if several coaches halt simultaneously, there can be queues for services). Coaches can be more flexible than trains – for instance, in an emergency, one waited while I made a phone call.

On some new services (called Rapide, Pullman, etc.), which are designed to provide a fast and non-stop service over long distances, there are such luxury touches as w.c. and wash-basin on board; hostess service of sandwiches or snacks and hot or refrigerated drinks; and films on video screens. If the coach is a double-decker, the films may be shown on the upper deck only.

The coaches are pretty punctual. I had only two significantly late arrivals in the course of writing this book (fewer than I had on a very much smaller number of train journeys). Most of my travelling was on National Express services. When very busy, NE sometimes hire coaches from other operators to supplement their own fleet and I found that these were not always up to the usual standard.

The Cost of Coach Travel

The table on p. 14 makes some comparisons with car and rail travel, correct when compiled but liable to change from time to time.

Whereas on trains you have to pay extra to reserve a seat, this is not the case on coaches. Should a National Express coach be full, every effort is made to provide alternative transport. If you have not booked a ticket, you may still be able to get on – provided that there are seats to spare.

Children under five travel free on National Express coaches. Those aged 5 to 17 get a third off the usual fare, so do students if they show their International Students Identity Card.

Overseas visitors can buy Britexpress passes. A pass entitles the user to unlimited travel on National Express and some other coaches on any five or ten days within a month (the pass is valid to sixty different towns); foreign students and members of the YHA are given a discount on these passes.

There are a number of cheap day-return tickets available, and some journeys into London are charged less than journeys from it: so make enquiries about what is available. On the other hand, late-night services may cost a bit more than day-time ones.

Because the low cost of coach travel is one of its biggest attractions, I have made a point of listing in each chapter of this book other money-savers too – accommodation bargains, cheap tickets for bussing around when you stay for a few days, and which sights are free. Some towns are remarkably good value, with plenty of free sights; others have few. One of this country's greatest assets is its huge number of city museums and art galleries, some of international renown and nearly all of them free. They often have live shows, from crafts to music recitals. Another is its cathedrals and their music (only Salisbury makes a fixed charge, but a donation is customary at others). And a third is our superb city parks, some of them huge and each with its own individuality, and often a concert at the bandstand – all free.

Things like season tickets of the National Trust, or the Historic Houses Assocation (which covers stately homes that are privately owned), show a saving only if there are several NT or

HHA properties in the area you intend to visit – and then only if they are open. (Most close in winter; many open only a few days a week.) The same applies to the Open to View ticket.

Here are eight tips for eating cheaply but well. (1) Picnics – the lists at the end of each chapter indicate good picnic sites. Or take a packed meal on the coach. (2) Buy Egon Ronay's *Just a Bite* guide, the best of several paperbacks on cheap eating places. (3) Fill up on the Great British Breakfast, and then a pub snack at lunchtime will be more than enough. (4) Ask the coach driver where the best fish-and-chippery is. (5) Ask the Tourist Information Centre whether the local technical college has a catering department where meals are to be had – in which case, you may get cordon bleu food at pub grub prices. (6) Local theatres, arts centres, craft centres and even cathedrals often have homemade food at very modest prices. (7) Department stores' restaurants cater for housewives who keep a keen eye on value. (8) Restaurants charging high prices for dinner often have very inexpensive lunches. Similarly, teas in the comfortable lounges of luxury hotels are often very inexpensive; such hotels frequently have low-price 'butteries' too.

Cost Comparisons

Note that: figures are for **two** adults; rail figures are for ordinary return tickets (valid for three months); coach figures are for period return (valid for 3 months); car figures are national average as calculated by the AA at 10.7p a mile – but petrol at motorway service stations costs about 4p more than elsewhere, and there are regional variations (in the west country, petrol is about 7p dearer than in Yorkshire, for instance). This figure should be doubled to allow for depreciation, tax, insurance and maintenance.

	Coach	Rail	Car
Leeds to Scarborough	£ 8.30	£18.00	£14.12
Birmingham to Newquay	£40.00	£72.00	£53.50
London to Newquay	£39.00	£85.00	£56.50
London to Bournemouth	£14.00	£32.60	£22.26
London to Eastbourne	£16.00	£21.60	£13.70
Maidstone to Newquay	£46.00	£99.40	£63.13
Maidstone to Bournemouth	£21.00	£46.40	£28.68

(Adapted from *Drive* magazine, July 1982)

Coach versus Car

Four out of ten people have no car. Of the other six, how many are now reluctant to use it for long journeys? This is not just to do with the price of petrol, or the depreciation which the mileometer inexorably records, but it also involves factors which are to do with pleasure.

A recent travel article describing King's Lynn said: 'You are met by roundabouts and bypasses, and traffic-flow experiments. It is a daunting introduction. A pestilential one-way system takes you away from the ancient core – better to park and discover it on foot.' When I visited King's Lynn, by coach, I had none of this hassle. I was free to look about me as the driver took the coach right into the centre, and set me down precisely where I wanted to be.

'But', say car drivers to me, 'don't you miss the convenience of a car for getting about if you stay several days in a town?' Not really. For a start, I am free of parking and one-way problems, which is a bonus. I invariably obtain a street plan before I arrive (by telephoning the town's Tourist Information Centre), which means that I don't waste time and effort on walking the wrong way to get to what interests me. Coaches (with very rare exceptions) put one down right where the action is; car parks are often on the perimeter of town, or involve going down and up multi-storey blocks.

At the end of each chapter, I have listed a selection of 'sights' very quickly reached by bus (or sometimes boat), the variety of which amply demonstrates that in each place there is plenty to see and do without need for a car – and that applies to all towns, not only those described in this book. In addition, in summer there are always coach excursions to be had.

Just as this book went to press, another was published which, although produced by the AA for car drivers, would be invaluable to anyone wanting to explore this country by coach. It is a directory called *The Book of British Towns* – nearly 700 of them. The design and content are admirable, with what is to be seen pithily tabulated. The clear, colourful street plans include (hurray!) the bus and coach stations. Not, perhaps, a book to carry with you for it weighs nearly

3½ lb., but an excellent journey planner if coupled with a National Express coach route map. The price is £11.95.

Activity Holidays by Coach

Increasingly, holidaymakers look for interesting activities to do – something more active than sightseeing. I have indicated which places have good walks or nature trails, for example, confining my suggestions to easy strolls, not the boot-and-backpack type of walking; and cycle hire is another option (or boat cruising, as at Oulton Broad, Lowestoft, for instance). But a good many activity holidays do not involve going about. A car might simply be an incubus – at the end of your stay, a flat battery and a fat bill for garaging perhaps?

The English Tourist Board and the regional boards (see list on p. 204) publish details of packages: accommodation plus activity under one roof and for one price. If, however, you want to go it alone, here are some suggestions (for fuller advice on where to go, telephone one of the boards; or, if you have decided on a destination, its Tourist Information Centre).

(1) There are plenty of pursuits which involve so little gear that no car is required to cart it about – simply choose a place which has the opportunity needed. Examples are: bird-watching, brass-rubbing, sketching.

(2) Other pursuits do need gear, but in many places it can be hired on arrival. Examples are: golf, sea-angling and underwater diving.

(3) For many people, shopping is an entertainment in itself – with bargains to be had at markets in particular, including the Women's Institutes' markets to which homemade produce is brought for sale. (At the end of each chapter, market days and early-closing days are listed.) Coaches will usually accept bulky purchases, to be stowed in the boot, up to the size of a suitcase.

(4) If you want a weekend of physical activity, choose a town with a good leisure centre where everything you want is under one roof; and book into a nearby hotel or guesthouse. The Sports Council (01-589 3411) can tell you where the best centres are.

(5) If you are more interested in music or the performing arts, choose a town with a week-long arts festival or a constant succession of concerts, plays, etc. (examples are Bath and Cheltenham); and, booking well ahead, select accommodation close by the centre where these happenings take place.

(6) Spectator sports are another diversion which needs no car. Regattas and water sports, for instance; or horse-racing: accessible by public transport – why pay to park a car that isn't needed? You will find I have mentioned, at the end of each chapter, when, as well as where, to find some such things going on.

Where to Stay

People often ask me what I do about accommodation, and about luggage, on my coach and bus travels. Many of the best places – all inexpensive – at which I have stayed are fully described in *Staying Off the Beaten Track*, a guide to well over a hundred small hotels, inns, farmhouses and the like. I have found that owners of farms and country houses are very willing to pick up coach travellers at their nearest town, often without making any charge; and so one gets both rural peace and lower prices than in town. Where this book is concerned, there is a list on p. 204 of the places at which I stayed.

These range from 'bargain breaks' at hotels which normally charge a lot, down to hostels. The latter have come up in the world lately, and now cater not just for backpackers but for families wanting basic comforts and good food. There is more information on pp. 205–6.

Outside term-time, universities often rent out student accommodation (with or without meals). To find out what may be available at your destination, telephone the British Universities Accommodation Consortium at Nottingham (0602 54571). Some universities also run Summer Schools which combine a little gentle learning with a holiday, and the moderate costs include accommodation. All year round, there are courses at other institutions which combine pleasurable activity with inexpensive bed-and-board: details from National Institute of Adult Education, 19(B) de Montfort Street, Leicester (send 80p).

Every autumn the English Tourist Board publishes a huge, free catalogue called 'Let's Go' which lists off-season bargain breaks throughout the country. Later it has a series of regional 'Spring into Summer' booklets with similar bargains from Easter to midsummer.

As to luggage, my nylon holdall, weighing a few ounces, accommodates enough for a week's travel, as follows: two loose-fitting dresses of drip-dry cotton which, like the one I wear, can be washed and dried overnight – flimsy Indian cottons are ideal. One change of underwear – also washable overnight. Flimsy nightie. Slippers (foldable but elegant ones) for evening wear. Washing gear in minimal cotton bag. In case the weather deteriorates: lightweight hooded showercoat, wool (not synthetic) cardigan, pants and gloves; but, on short trips, phoning for a weather forecast obviates such contingency planning (the numbers to dial are given in the front of telephone directories). All this lot is easily kept in order by rolling each up and securing it with a rubber-band. If my bedroom has no bathroom of its own, the showercoat doubles as a dressing-gown. Where things like toothpaste, talc or cosmetics are concerned, I pack the minimum sizes and choose plastic packs rather than metal or glass. I also pack a 100W light bulb for reading in bed (many hotel lamps are 40W). The total weight is under 6lb. And I don't need to cart the holdall around: coach stations have left-luggage offices.

When and Where to Go

Spring and autumn are ideal times although services may be fewer than in summer. (In high summer, coaches – like everything else – may be crowded, and hot when stationary; and charges go up in many hotels.) Since coaches can be heated, winter holidays, too, have a lot to be said for them, if you choose a destination where plenty of sights remain open all the year round and where there are winter events (towns with theatres and cathedrals are a good choice then): I've given information about all this at the end of each chapter. Provincial theatres are not to be despised. You may find

West End artistes in a production opening later in London; or hear Janet Baker, for instance, singing at much closer range than in London's huge Festival Hall. An easy way to find out what's on where is to buy *The Times* on Saturday which always has a supplement previewing the week ahead, nationwide.

In choosing where to go for the purposes of this book, I deliberately assorted my destinations. I included some of the world-famous places which all first-time visitors want to see – Canterbury and Cheltenham, for instance. But there are others with almost as great interest which deserve to be better known – one example is Sherborne, and Shrewsbury is another.

Because the big 'Maritime England' promotion is focusing attention on the shoreline, I have included several coastal resorts – a colourful free pamphlet 'To the Sea by Bus' includes a route map of coach services – send a stamped envelope to National Bus Co., 172 Buckingham Palace Road, London SW1W 9TN.

I've also made a point of including a number of cities not ordinarily thought of as tourist spots; the great industrial centres. For things are not what they used to be. Many of them have in recent years woken up to the fact that they have a history; that they have hotels used by businessmen midweek but quiet – and cheaper – from Friday to Sunday; that they have shops and shows – in short, that they have a lot to offer tourists – and they are now going out of their way to entertain them. At the end of the book are details of some very interesting weekend 'packages', ideal for coach travellers; to track down other such packages, enquire from the various tourist boards.

And what easier way than a coach for joining one's spouse, after he/she has done a hard week's conferring in Sheffield or Bradford, say, for a weekend of relaxation together there?

What Every Traveller Should Know

The English Tourist Board issues a free booklet listing the 600 or so Tourist Information Centres throughout the country. Get one! This is the open sesame to all sorts of ideas. Pick your destination, ring the TIC (long-distance telephoning is cheaper on Saturdays) and they will tell all – how to get there, what to see and do, where to stay or eat. All your problems solved. (ETB's address is on p. 204.)

At your hotel, tune in to the local radio station in the morning – for news of travel services, what's on and the weather.

For the best country walks, join the Ramblers Association (it also has a bed-and-breakfast guide): 1 Wandsworth Road, London SW8. For the best town walks (largely away from traffic, and with a minimum of wasted time), either ask the Tourist Information Centre for a 'trail' leaflet; or go round with an expert guide – in a party (free, or for a small fee) or on your own (usually a fee of a few pounds, but particularly well worth it if you have a specialised interest – such as Thomas Hardy in Salisbury or pubs in Brighton). Car tours cost far more, of course.

Guides vary in quality, but I found that most whose services I tried were excellent – doubling the interest of the visit. Some wear a blue badge indicating that they have been trained to tourist board standards (many are fluent in several languages) but I found excellent unbadged guides too, imparting knowledge not to be had from guidebooks. Only one treated her audience like a class of dimwits.

To keep the children entertained while you do your own thing, enquire what children's sessions or quiz sheets are on offer at the local museum, art gallery, library or theatre (often free). Play parks are usually free and may have a play leader in charge. Older children can safely be left in leisure centres.

Lonely? Meet local like-minded people by enquiring what clubs have meetings (for Scrabble, over-18s, folk song, wildlife, archaeology, bridge, organ-playing – you name it). Almost invariably, visitors are welcomed, and usually without charge.

You may find tourist boards curiously ignorant about which recommended 'sights' in their area are accessible by coach or bus, in which case you will have to turn to the coach or bus companies for further information. One honourable exception is the Heart of England Tourist Board (see p. 204) which sells a first-rate paperback of *Places to Visit* (in Gloucestershire, Worcestershire, Shropshire and Staffordshire) which has a bus symbol against every place accessible by bus or coach: a huge number.

About booklets from Tourist Information Centres. Overseas visitors can often obtain leaflets in their own language if they enquire; and Centres often collect information helpful to disabled visitors. It is likely to double what you get out of a visit if you write off for a guidebook and town plan to study in the coach before you arrive.

Note The destinations described in this book were reached from a variety of starting points, simply depending upon where I happened to be. Obviously, each can be approached from a number of other directions too.

Because things like opening hours, prices and services are constantly changing, the information in this book should be regarded as only an approximate guide. For the latest facts, telephone the nearest Tourist Information Centre; which will be able to tell you of other local sightseeing possibilities and recreations, in addition to those I have listed.

TO BRIGHTON

from South London

Coaches depart about 16 times a day and the journey takes
about 1½ hours (or 2½ hours from central London). It goes
through countryside and up into the South Downs.

That ceaseless 18th-century traveller, William Cobbett, said of
Brighton: 'It is so situated that a coach which leaves it not very early
in the morning reaches London by noon. Great parcels of stock-
jobbers skip backwards and forwards.'

They skip even faster on today's coaches; and it did not take
me long to shed the industrial outskirts of London and, passing the
old Croydon Aerodrome buildings which conservationists are now
eager to preserve as part of aviation history, to speed out towards
the countryside. From a leafy road that runs high up, there were far
views ahead. The coach sped through Purley's outskirts – suburban
gardens were at their spring best, with magnolias and pink cherry
blossom bursting out all over, purple aubretia pouring from walls
and rockery banks, or scarlet tulips standing to attention like
grenadiers.

Once beyond Coulsdon and across the boundary into Surrey,
the scenery became rural, with horses grazing in the fields. On a
dual carriageway and with urban congestion behind, the coach
picked up speed (overtaking everyone else on the road). We
zoomed over the top of London's orbital motorway (M25) that
crossed beneath us, and made our way south – following a route that
wound its way up and down among green hills, golden gorse and
silver hawthorn on the roadside banks, fields of grazing cows
alternating with woods of larch and birch.

The coach made a detour to pick up passengers from Crawley,
riding in at treetop level through woodlands to reach a very modern

town centre of new supermarket and polytechnic blocks, but made more attractive by their surroundings of flowerbeds and park. The coach paused here amongst the smooth lawns and the beds of tulips, and with churches ancient and modern in view; then it turned back, via a roundabout of brilliant heather and that leafy road again, to resume its journey.

There is a colourful book, no bigger than a pack of cigarettes, which I often carry in my handbag: Collins' *Gem Guide – Trees*. Out it came along the next stretch of the ride, for the wide strip separating the two carriageways is full of chestnuts, conifers and other trees in great variety.

The ploughed fields that followed were chalky-pale (we were on the edge of the chalk hills of the South Downs) with pottering crows sharply silhouetted against them. Already the lambs in the meadows were half-grown. Ahead lay the Downs, their smoky-blue humps like the backs of whales. Farm buildings and churches hereabouts are (typically of a chalk region) flint-walled; and some houses are tile-hung in Sussex style. The road led onwards to little Pyecombe, the sign with its name bearing a shepherd's crook because once this village had a forge celebrated for making these crooks (and, later, for making bishops' crooks). Its tiny church stands on the brow of the hill. Past the Plough Inn (with old plough outside) are the white stone pillars that mark the boundary of Sussex – and of Brighton. The traffic began to build up here.

This leafy road makes a fine approach to the town. Houses with pretty gardens are succeeded by a particularly beautiful park with a row of delicate fountain-jets, and flowerbeds that produced gasps of admiration from several coach passengers. To the left is Preston Manor (of which more later) and to the right a rather distinguished Youth Hostel (see list at end), with sports centre nearby. Every summer, a design for each flowerbed in this park is sent in by a different town with which Brighton has associations – all vying to produce something even more attractive than the others. The rockery on the right of the road is laid out like the picture on willow-pattern plates, floodlit at night.

And so into the heart of Brighton: the Grand Parade. When the Prince Regent built his summer Pavilion here, this is where the court paraded in all their finery. Regency houses – bow fronts, lacey ironwork – fringe the area, and its centre consists of lawns, flowers and statuary: still an elegant oasis in the heart of what is now a considerable city.

There was a quick glimpse of the sea, of Palace Pier and of the Pavilion's oriental domes before the coach swung round to squeeze itself through a narrow lane and come to rest in Pool Valley, only a few minutes behind schedule.

Regency Vanities

It was really Dr Richard Russell who, in writing his 'Dissertation Concerning the Use of Sea Water' (1785), put what was once a muddy little fishing village onto the map (he lived where the Royal

Albion Hotel now stands), though it took the Prince Regent to make it fashionable – first by coming to Brighton in pursuit of the good doctor's 'cure' himself (he was a great believer in the properties of both bathing in and drinking sea-water); then by installing his beloved Mrs Fitzherbert in a house – now a YMCA hostel – overlooking the parade; and ultimately by building that most exotic of royal palaces – the oriental Pavilion. Around this grew up all the pleasures his courtiers could desire. The coach station (sited where the Prince had a muddy pool drained and paved) is right in the middle of all this, nicely sandwiched between the sea and the Pavilion, close by the famous Lanes. Therefore it is easy for a coach traveller to spend an entire day exploring these parts (and often this is all that tourists do, even though there is far more to Brighton).

The Pavilion is all fantasy: Indian without and Chinese within. Much of the original furniture is there, and what furniture it is! – carved into the shape of dolphins and sphinxes, dragons and birds, with hardly ever a simple chair- or table-leg to be seen. In recent years, grime has been removed to reveal all the original, dazzling colours. It was almost a relief after wandering through this succession of magnificent and exotic rooms to enter the kitchens where row upon row of huge copper pans and an enormous spit were standing ready, as if for yet another banquet that night. In summer the banqueting room has its gold plate laid out on its table, part of the annual Regency Exhibition.

From this dreamlike and brilliant world, I wandered to The Lanes, a cobweb of tiny, brick-paved walks (no cars) where little shops, pubs and restaurants jostle one another – selling antiques (Queen Mary used to hunt for finds here), crafts, pretty clothes or tempting food. The goods may differ from those of the Prince Regent's times but the atmosphere is much the same – vanity fair!

I walked up past the Theatre Royal (a pretty, plush-and-gilt Victorian theatre where, on a previous visit, I'd enjoyed Penelope Keith in a play later to become a West End success – Brighton is often one jump ahead of London's theatregoers) to the Indian-style dome that had once been the royal stables with riding school adjoining. Now part of this houses Brighton's museum – a very unusual one, and not only because of the splendid building in which it is housed, where even the entrance is a grandiose and golden Indian arch. It has probably the only major collection of *art nouveau* and *art deco* in the country (furniture, dresses and jewelry), and also galleries with other specialised collections. In one, the history of the seaside is the theme; in another (the most dramatic of all, I thought) is a collection of outstanding ethnic art, spotlit against a dark background; and one traces the area's history back to 100 million years ago, beginning with a fossilised mammoth tusk superimposed on a full-scale picture of the huge creature. Brighton is surrounded by hills where its earliest, Celtic inhabitants built their forts and villages: small-scale models recreate these vividly. The story is then taken on in other exhibits, with finds from Roman, Saxon and mediaeval times.

Beside the Seaside: Beaches, Lawns and Harbour
Back then to the coach and bus station, for a ride westward along the seafront. Buses no. 700, 230 and 730 go all the way to adjoining Portslade-by-Sea (3 miles away), following the seafront all the time. A ride like this is a good way to see what the resort has to offer, with the intention of returning later to chosen spots. In summer, there are illuminations all the way along to Hove.

Most people simply stay near the centre and Palace Pier, but beyond West Pier (at present closed) lies quieter Hove, and here everything changes.

But before getting to West Pier, I looked out for the Old Ship Hotel because it has an interesting story. When Charles II (then prince) was attempting to escape the Roundheads by fleeing across the Channel, he was aided by a Sussex skipper called Tettersell. He later rewarded him with money to buy the Old Ship and become an innkeeper. Every year, the Old Ship sponsors a cross-Channel yacht race to commemorate the royal escape, and nearly a hundred sailing-boats gather along this stretch of coast for the start of the race.

In Hove there are fewer high-rise flats and more splendours of early Victorian architecture, carefully conserved. Corinthian pilasters rise, three stories high, to stately pediments. After Regency Square, where striped canopies shelter the pretty balconies of the smaller hotels, there comes Brunswick Square, followed by the lovely curve of Adelaide Crescent which leads to Palmeira Square (now full of offices and English language schools for overseas youngsters). These have carefully tended gardens in which to sun one's self, or picnic, when the incoming tide has partly covered the pebbly beaches. Up in Palmeira Square, the time is told by a floral clock (the bachelors' buttons were doing so more accurately than the nearby church clock). Beach-huts and seafront lawns follow (with bowling, croquet and suchlike): the West End Restaurant here almost has its feet in the sea.

After that, it seems as if the seaside has vanished, and nose-in-air motorists zip by the next bit as fast as they can in order to escape the view of factories and power station. But appearances are deceptive, and locals know what lies behind and how easily it is reached if you get off the bus at the Schooner Inn (which, incidentally, has a bar with snacks that overlooks an absorbing water-front spectacle). For this is where the basin of Shoreham Harbour lies, and it is easy to walk across the tops of the triple lock-gates to get to the other side of the basin and to the little-used beaches that are nearby. The basin is frequented not only by great tankers and cargo-ships, best seen when they move in or out at high tide, but by the small sailing-boats of the local yacht club. Alongside are bonded warehouses for sherry shipped in from Spain and stacks of timber from the Baltic. When the tide is out, the beach beyond is the place to be, for then the sand is revealed. Having only one café and shop, this beach is mercifully free of litter as well as crowds.

There is a view from here of Shoreham's harbour close by. Two stone breakwaters shelter the mouth of the River Adur (pronounced Ada), and when I was there a dredger was busy shifting the river's silt away. It's an interesting spot with a light-house, lifeboat house (sometimes open to the public), old fort with ramparts to walk upon, and coastguards' lookout – you may be allowed in when they're not busy. The best part, the west jetty, is reached by a somewhat roundabout bus trip (no. 21 and 22).

Beside the Seaside: Clifftops and Marina

The best way to travel the eastward stretch of seafront is to go first to Rottingdean by the inland route (bus no. 2), and come back along the coast by another bus (several services, some open-topped in summer) which is then on the side of the road close to the sea. Half-way back (at the Marina), you could change onto Volks' quaint seafront railway if you prefer.

The quiet heart of this one-time smuggling village, tucked away from the main road, is charming: Rottingdean has smooth lawns with beautiful houses of flint or half-timbering, a pond and a wide green (suitable for picnics) overlooked by the old Plough Inn. Byways are cobbled; the main street has a number of hotels and inns. There is access to the beach through a gap in the cliffs beyond.

A number of celebrities have lived at Rottingdean. Sir Edward Burne-Jones was one (he designed the stained glass in the church), and his nephew Kipling later lived here too – perhaps it was Rottingdean that inspired his poem about smuggling, '. . . brandy for the parson, baccy for the clerk', because the local vicar, Hooker, is known to have colluded with the smugglers. Hooker, whose pupils included Bulwer Lytton and Cardinal Manning, has his bust in the church, and his house is now a museum of toys – with paintings by William Nicholson, who lived there later.

The fast ride back into Brighton is a splendid clifftop route, white cliffs contrasting with green tops. We sped past a windmill on the right and the huge buildings of Roedean girls' school, and then the Marina came into sight far below on the left – so huge it is almost a seaport in its own right. There are often historic ships there among the throng of small sailing-boats, every week has a special event like a regatta or race, and one can buy fresh fish and oysters from the fish farm (or eat them in the restaurant).

Approaching Brighton from this direction, one passes architecture of a slightly younger vintage than on the west side. Lord Olivier is one of many theatrical people who have lived here, in the terraces of houses with bow fronts and canopied verandahs, big windows and delicate ironwork.

Within minutes, the bus was back in the centre of things again and I got out by the historic aquarium, where sea-lions and dolphins live an underground life, to take one last look at the seafront from Palace Pier. Things were much the same as in 1736 when a parson on holiday wrote home: 'My morning business is bathing in the sea, and then buying fish, and my evening occupation is riding out for air and counting the ships.' Thousands do much the same things today.

SOME MORE PLACES TO VISIT

For bus times and route map, tel. 0273 606600. Many routes go up into the South Downs or by the sea.

Booth Museum (buses no. 10, 11, 35). Good bird museum, facing a pretty park.

+Bramber and Beeding (bus. no. 100). Villages with flint or half-timbered cottages and pretty inns. Bramber has castle ruins, butterfly museum in a great Tudor house, and a museum of pipes for smokers. Cafés.

+Devils Dyke (bus no. 77, open-top, summer only). High windswept hill, 45-mile panorama of four counties within view. Can walk down to Fulking, see below; or watch hang-gliders. Café.

Engineerium (bus no. 16). Victorian pumping station – in action on Sundays – and museum: hundreds of models.

+Falmer (buses no. 128, 728, 729). This village, where Godfrey Wynn lived, has a large green and pond full of wildfowl.

+Fulking (bus no. 106, infrequent). A lovely downland drive, passing the Shepherd and Dog Inn (good food) with stream and a tiled spring with text ('He sendeth springs into the valleys . . .').

Hove Museum (buses no. 1, 6). Of great excellence. Modern art, porcelain, toys, etc.

+Hove Park (buses no. 3a, 11, 16, 29, 229). Many acres of lawns and roses.

+Lancing (bus no. 229 to Sussex Pad Hotel). Short but uphill rural walk to cathedral-like chapel of the College:

spectacular rose window, seen best about an hour before sunset. Can also walk from Sussex Pad (good food) to Old Shoreham by riverside footpath and over old trestle bridge.

+Old Shoreham (buses no. 2, 100, 229). Behind the Red Lion – lunches served in garden – are a pretty church and lane; and steep track up to a fine viewpoint on Mill Hill.

+Preston Manor (many bus services). Elegant mansion with Edwardian furniture and a 'lived in' look. Garden.

Shoreham (many bus services). Marlipins Museum in the High Street; fishermen's 18th-century cottages in back streets.

+Stanmer Park (buses no. 25, 128, 729). Acres of grass and trees, weekend cricket, spectacular blossom in May, pond with swans. Museum of rural implements, including well with horsewheel. Farm. Café. The campus of Sussex University adjoins and is open to visitors: fine views.

+Steyning (bus no. 100 – continuation of Bramber route). Beautiful street of jutting, half-timbered houses and Georgian ones, pretty gardens spilling onto cobbled road, craft shops, restaurants, fine church and a big green.

+Withdean Park (go by bus no. 46 to Peacock Lane; walk downhill and return by buses no. 5, 5a, 5b). Roses, irises and over a hundred varieties of lilac in acres of park with hardly anyone about. No w.c. near.

All the sights I have described can be visited nearly every day of the year, except for (summer only) Volks' railway, Shoreham Museum, power station.

SOME ANNUAL EVENTS

Jan. Vienna Ice Revue. **March** Historic Motor Cycles Rally. **April** Southern Garden Show. **May** Horse-Driving Trials (often with Duke of Edinburgh). Arts Festival. Boat Show. 'Royal Escape' Yacht Race. **July** Antiques Fair. Carnival in Preston Park. Open day of Brighton's nursery garden and citrus house. **Aug.** Regatta. Brighton Races. **Sept.** National Speed Trials. **Oct.** Women's International Tennis. **Nov.** Veteran Car Run.

TOURIST INFORMATION CENTRES

54 Old Steine (0273 23755, weekends, 26450).

Kings Road (0273 26450).

Town Hall, Hove (0273 775400)

Publications obtainable from the Centres include: Brighton and Hove: Things to See and Do (10p); street map (45p – the free bus map is just as detailed); A Walk Around the Best of Brighton (free); You Can Get It in Brighton – shopping guide (£1.50); restaurant list (free); Guide for Disabled Visitors (free); In and Around Sussex (40p); events lists – racing, music, sports, etc. (free).

The Centre has times of bus tours, boat trips and coach excusions. These include a summer open-top tour of the city; and an escorted 3-hour tour of its environs, in a closed-top double-decker. There is a leaflet about guided private tours (in car) by the Brighton Personal Guide Service (0273 504034); and details of cycle hire.

ECONOMY TIPS   Accommodation

Brighton has a free Take a Break book-let which includes some bargain breaks. Youth Hostel: Patcham Place, London Road. **Transport** Bargainride is a cheap day-return bought on buses. It is valid for trips over 3 miles (each way) at off-peak times. A travel card valid for a week gives unlimited travel over a wide area, covering all the places I've described above except Bramber, Fulking and Steyning.

On Sundays and public holidays, a day-long bus ticket entitles one adult and one child to go anywhere in the same area as the travel card.

Day Explorer tickets (see p. 206) take you further afield: to Singleton (open-air museum), Chichester, Bognor, Arundel, Littlehampton, Sheffield Park (steam railway), Tunbridge Wells, Drusilla's Zoo Park, Eastbourne, Pevensey and Hastings. **Admissions** Of the sights I have described the following are free: Brighton Museum, Hove Museum, Booth Museum, power station, lifeboat house, Bramber Castle ruins, Lancing College chapel, Marlipins Museum, Stanmer Park (and museum). Explorer ticket entitles you to a discount on entrance fees to various places.

MARKET DAYS 'Flea market', Saturdays. Open-air market. daily – fresh fish, etc.

LOCAL ALE Raven.

TO BURY ST EDMUNDS
from Lowestoft

Coaches depart approximately 3 times a day, and the journey
takes about 1½ hours. It passes through rich farming country,
with a succession of pretty villages along the way. A good stop
on the route would be Beccles (for its waterside paths and
gardens; regatta in August).

This journey was the only one that involved me in a serious delay.
The local company's coach (from Yarmouth) simply did not turn
up! Apparently, its driver, to make up for time lost earlier in his
journey, decided to cut Lowestoft out of his route, so there I waited
in vain. After much telephoning, a car belonging to the coach
company was sent from Yarmouth to carry me to Bury – which I
therefore reached two hours late.

The first part of the route is a straight, fast road (between
fields, golf course and woods) to Beccles, a market town dominated
by the pale grey, 100-foot, detached tower of its church, and by a
half-dozen maltings standing in a cluster. Around its Market Square
are little Georgian houses with dormers or pantiled roofs. The River
Waveney (a pretty sight, with willows, ducks and boats) marks the
border between Suffolk and Norfolk.

Beyond here, the marshy land is low-lying – its peaty soil
drained by dykes which wildfowl frequent. Willows border the
road. As we drove westward, there was a succession of streams, flint
churches, crimson roses on whitewashed walls and fields of dozing
cows or sugar beet separated by hedges with immense trees (oak
and ash, mainly).

Around Bungay's central feature, an octagonal market house
with pretty cupola, stalls were spread out. This is a town of mature
brick or colourwashed houses, inns with eye-catching signs and
decorative wrought iron.

We crossed river after river, and sped by fields of golden grain flecked with poppies or of knee-high grass, then of potatoes – stretching for miles, as far as the eye could see. The size of the fields (and the barns) became immense: at one point the scene was prairie-like, an entire plain filled with wheat.

The church towers along this route were varied – from simple round ones or small hexagons, to huge pinnacled edifices carefully designed from knapped flints contained within a framework of finely dressed white stone. Billingford has an impressive windmill, Scole its great inn of red brick dated 1655 and with Dutch-style gables, Palgrave is pretty with black-and-white houses, at Wortham thatchers were at work, while in Rotesdale – a very long village – every house seemed to be a different colour (various pinks, terra-cottas and greens); some were extra colourful with wistaria too.

Between the villages, there were high hedges and verges to enjoy – summer's wildflowers major on pinks, reds and mauves by contrast with the white and yellow of spring. Long, luxuriant grass, set swaying by the speed of passing traffic, flashed silvery in the afternoon light.

Ixworth is possibly the prettiest village along this route: a place of leaded windows, hanging flower baskets, and shining brass doorknockers beneath the porches. Roofs were mossy; façades of brick, or oxblood-coloured stucco, or pargetted plaster – some half-hidden by Virginia creeper.

Another windmill, and yet another river (filled with yellow waterlilies), and so on through still lovely scenery – woodland and pastures, flint-and-thatch villages with carved and colourful name-boards, rows of limes or chestnuts – until we came to Bury itself. The road into the town centre passed a terrace of dark green cottages with a dozen steps up to each front door and then some half-timbered houses. To the left were the colossal stone walls of the abbey, supported by great buttresses. The coach station is behind the Market Square and right beside Bury's local museum, which is housed in ancient Moyses Hall, a good place to visit before exploring the town.

Martyrdom, Miracles, Murders and Magna Carta

Moyses Hall was so-called after its first owner. Clearly Moyses prospered, for his house was large, built of stone and has survived the years well. In the Norman undercroft, there is now a museum of local life – from mediaeval stone coffins and crossbows to the penny-farthings and barrel-organs of not so long ago. When I called, a party of schoolchildren with quiz-sheets were more interested, though, in Bury's celebrated murderer and his victim, 'Maria Marten of the Red Barn', to whom a section is devoted; and in the gibbet on which in previous times executed bodies were hung to rot. Plastic badges of Corder, the murderer, and death-masks sell briskly at the souvenir stall – where you can also buy traditional clay pipes with motifs as varied as Fred Archer's head or skull-and-crossbones.

Outside is the Georgian Market Cross building (designed by Adam – now an art gallery), and a mixture of others, old and new. Urns and garlands are on one façade, decorative pargetting on another, which also has historic figures including St Edmund himself. Brutally slain and beheaded in 869 by marauding Vikings, the body of the youthful King Edmund was brought to the monastery here for burial – upon which miraculous cures at his shrine began to be reported. When the Viking Knut (Canute) ultimately conquered much of England, he compensated the monks for the previous devastation; and later monarchs, doing homage at the shrine, added still further to their rights and riches – hence the increased splendour of the abbey by Norman times, and of the town which the monks then laid out (on a grid pattern) outside it. Wide Churchgate Street, for instance, was the processional way to the shrine. The town and abbey were protected by high walls on three sides and by the river on the fourth. The abbey became a cultural centre (its illuminated manuscripts and other treasures are scattered among the great museums of the world), while the town became rich from the sale of wool cloth and farm produce.

But the prospering citizens began to resent the monks' dictatorship, and the story of bloody deeds in the 13th and 14th centuries makes riveting reading: townsmen looted the abbey, monks slayed the townsfolk while in church, there were mass hangings, an abbot was kidnapped and ransomed, the Black Death took a heavy toll, followed by Jack Straw's rebellion, a prior and monks were murdered and punitive fines exacted before the town and the abbey learned how to live in harmony.

I wandered among the ancient sidestreets (Cornhill, The Traverse, Guildhall Street) which had once seen riots more violent than at Toxteth. Now they are relatively quiet roads with shops where one can buy crafts or curios and studios of silversmiths and glass engravers. The old Corn Exchange is here (you can watch the dealings on Wednesdays), 17th-century Cupola House, the tiny Nutshell pub (smallest in England?), and Georgian or older homes. Wide Abbeygate Street is a good shopping centre with a fine vista: Ridleys, the grocers, have been here for generations, and my purchases were handed to me in a bag reproducing their advertisement for Christmas 1895 ('. . . toy bonbons, ornamental biscuits in elegant tins . . . Confidential orders will receive special attention').

At the foot of the street is the wide square of Angel Hill, with the impressive abbey gateway opposite, built in 1347 to replace an earlier one destroyed by rioters: portcullis and arrow-slits show that the monks did not intend their new gateway to suffer the same fate. Around this square are a Clock Museum (in a Queen Anne house owned by the National Trust), the handsome Angel Hotel (a coaching inn when Dickens described it in *Pickwick Papers*), and the 18th-century Athenaeum (its elegant Adam-style assembly rooms still used for various functions) with a charming passageway of pink and green cottages beside it.

So much for secular Bury – now I turned to what is left of the monastery which once made the town great. Today there is little but ruins, surrounded by acres of tranquil gardens: groves, stumps of ancient walls, paths leading down to one of Bury's rivers, the Lark (the other is called, charmingly, the Linnet), pets' corner, café and a rose garden enclosed within yew hedges, which American visitors always seek out. It was given by an American author, one of many Americans based near here during the Second World War (his book, *Suffolk Summer*, can be bought at the Tourist Information

Centre, which opens up in the abbey gardens every summer).

One often hears American voices in Bury. As a great many Puritans emigrated from Suffolk to America, their genealogically minded descendants head for the town because the county's record office is here. The presidential White House is built of bricks made at Woolpit near Bury. I sat on a metal bench made from an American 'Flying Fortress' to enjoy the scent of all those roses before exploring further, and to reflect on times past in this historic spot.

St Edmund's silver and gold shrine vanished long ago: it was destroyed in a 15th-century fire. Then the rebuilt abbey (which must have been very colourful for there are descriptions of its painted roof, hangings, stained glass and fourteen altars) was largely destroyed by Henry VIII, who looted most of its treasures too. The graves of several abbots survived – and the momentous site where, on a November day in 1214, Cardinal Langton and the barons gathered to swear at the high altar that they would force King John to agree to Magna Carta as, indeed, they did at Runnymede the following June. A stone was set there in 1847 which reads:

> Where the rude buttress totters to its fall,
> And ivy mantles o'er the crumbling wall . . .
> Still we read in deathless records how
> The high-soul'd priest confirm'd the barons' vow:
> And FREEDOM, unforgetful, still recites
> This second birthplace of our native RIGHTS.

There also survived the tremendous span of the abbey's west front – now pierced by sash and bay windows, for houses were built behind it – from which one can look across the green where Elisabeth Frink's 'St Edmund' stands, and directly through the other great Norman gatetower to the processional route of Churchgate Street.

The church to the right of the green (St James's) is Tudor, extended in the 20th century after it was given cathedral status. The superb nave was the work of John Wastell who designed King's College Chapel, Cambridge. On entering, the church seems to be a sea of blue – a thousand needlepoint kneelers are propped up in the pews, each stitched with an emblem of the school or parish which provided it. This is altogether a colourful church – angels of blue, scarlet and gold soar on high and in the very lovely chapel of St Edmund children have made a long tapestry with scenes from his life.

Out into the sunlight once more, to walk past the overgrown tombstones and mediaeval charnel house (to accommodate bones exhumed by later burials) in order to reach an older church, St Mary's, at the corner of the abbey grounds, and to look at its famous hammerbeam roof with a procession of dark oak angels bearing incense and candles towards the altar.

The body of Henry VIII's sister was re-interred here after he destroyed its original resting place, the abbey itself. The tombstone is plain – unlike that of a local worthy, John Barnet, who long before he died in 1467 had his own bony cadaver carved and sited near his pew. Above is a more cheerful ceiling with emblems associated with him, decorated with flecks of looking-glass and the pious hope 'Grace me govern, God me guide'. The scent of stocks and pinks hung in the air, and the organ was playing softly.

Later, the curfew bell would sound. A draper was lost in the woods one night but St Mary's bell guided him home, so he gave money for a regular curfew bell. Another benefactor, Jankyn Smith, is remembered with a service and an annual distribution of 'cakes and ale' at the Guildhall which he gave to the town.

From here it is only a short stroll to the Theatre Royal, one of the few Regency theatres still surviving (it belongs to the National Trust), and then easily back to the coach station; for the early town planning of the monks means that Bury was and still is a neat and compact town, ideal for anyone to explore on foot.

SOME MORE PLACES TO VISIT

West Suffolk Public Transport Guide has times and route maps of the area (obtainable from the coach station, or tel. 0284 66171). Bus routes to the north go through undulating countryside with forests. To the south the scenery is even more varied.

+Euston (buses no. 905–6). Euston Hall; and a walk along Duke's Ride to catch bus back. This is in the Breckland area, sandy heathland with villages of thatched cottages along the way. The 18th-century Hall, with park landscaped by William Kent, has a café. Interesting church.

+Hardwick Park (buses no. 951, 952). Heath, exceptionally fine cedars.

Haverhill (buses no. 931–6). Sports centre, market, few old houses. Along with all the usual sports facilities there are a golf net, rifle range and climbing wall.

Honington (buses no. 903, 904, 906, 908). 1½-mile walk to Ixworth Thorpe: small thatched church. Likely to see Harriers and Tornados flying overhead. Further along this route is Sapiston: pretty village with watermill on river.

Horringer (buses no. 931–936). Pretty village. Alight here for walks in deer park of Ickworth House. The house (full of art treasures) is 1 mile from entrance: a Georgian palace (National Trust). Café. There is a crafts centre in the village.

+Ixworth (buses no. 912–18). Abbey remains, timbered buildings. Pakenham working windmill open to the public

and, a ¾-mile walk, a working watermill.

Lavenham (Chambers' or Rules bus). Preserved mediaeval wool town with weavers' half-timbered cottages, inns, guildhall, fine church. You may hear the local handbell-ringers there.

Long Melford (many services). Beautyspot village. Melford Hall (National Trust) and Kentwell Hall. Tremendous church. Long green (with a fair in summer).

Newmarket (buses no. 940–7). Racing centre – with a new museum of horseracing.

Stowmarket (buses no. 924–5). Museum of East Anglian Life in mediaeval barn; watermill, smithy, etc.: 29 acres of exhibits.

+West Stow (bus no. 903). For a pretty forest walk of 3 miles to Lackford; return on bus no. 974 or 975.

Most of the above places can be visited nearly every day throughout the year but the following close in the winter: Ickworth House, Euston Hall, Ixworth Abbey, Clare's Ancient House, Pakenham Watermill, Horringer Crafts Centre, Lavenham Guildhall and Little Hall, Melford Hall, Kentwell Hall, Museum of East Anglian Life.

SOME ANNUAL EVENTS

June Book Fair. Carnival. Music Festival. Cake-and-ale service. **Sept.** Tree Fair (Rougham) – accessible by bus. **Oct.** Harvest festival at cathedral, with Lord Lieutenant, borough mayors, etc. **Nov.** Antiques Fair. **Dec.** Carols by candlelight in cathedral.

(free); footpath map of Bury St Edmunds (40p).

The Centre has times of guided walks, coach tours, cycle hire and Morris dancing displays.

To find out where you can see thatchers at work, tel. 028 489 210.

TOURIST INFORMATION CENTRE

Abbey Garden in summer (0284 64667– at other times, 0284 63233)

Publications obtainable from the Centre include: Tourist Pack, containing mini-guide, town plan, town trail, where to eat, where to stay, where to go (60p); events lists, free; official guide – hardback book with excellent text and colour photos (£1.15); Abbey guidebook (40p.); leisure facilities booklet

ECONOMY TIPS

Accommodation Some hotels offer bargain breaks. **Transport** Anywhere ticket provides unlimited bus travel in the Eastern Counties region for a day. There are (on Tuesdays) cheap returns; also economical 10-trip tickets. **Admissions** Of the places mentioned, the following are free: Abbey ruins, Theatre Royal (when not in use), Clock Museum, a regimental museum, Corn

Exchange, Clare Priory and country park, Ickworth Park.

EARLY-CLOSING DAY Thursday.

MARKET DAYS Street market, Wednesdays and Saturdays. Cattle market, Wednesdays.

LOCAL ALE & FOOD Greene King ale. Suffolk-cured ham. Honey.

TO CANTERBURY
from Brighton

A new cross-country coach route running twice daily, three days a week. The journey takes 2¾ hours and goes through an area of outstanding natural beauty: the hills and valleys of the Weald and of the North Downs. Lewes, Tenterden or Wye would be a good place to make a day-long stop on the way.

The coach route out of Brighton passes the Royal Engineers' barracks, Moulsecoomb Wild Park, then Stanmer Park (see p. 30) and the very modern university buildings up on their hilltop. We were soon out into the countryside – sometimes passing among trees that made a leafy roof over the road, sometimes rising out of valleys to enjoy uninterrupted views far over the Weald. Lambs, chalky fields and spring blossom made a typically Sussex scene. A couple of bold crows pottered on the grassy verge of the road quite unperturbed by the passing traffic.

Lewes was quickly reached. We entered past the flint-walled prison which looks like a castle, glimpsed beyond cherry blossom, and down a steep old road lined with a great variety of houses – tile-hung, flint or weatherboarded, some very colourful and many with elegant doorways or balconies. The Norman castle high on its mound is tucked away down a sidestreet – just one of many ancient buildings that it would take hours to explore in this most historic of towns. Leaving Lewes there was a quick glimpse of the old 18th-century brewery by the waterside, and then we were once more back on the fast road heading towards Ringmer where tile-hung or thatched houses stand around a large cricket green. Nearby is a well with a wheel to pump up the water.

The road ahead was one long, straight line stretching to the horizon and beyond – originally laid down by the Romans. Delicate mauve ladies' smocks thronged the sides of ditches outside the fields of Raystede animal rescue centre. Beyond farm buildings and streams near Halland, gliders were coming in to land. There was great variety all along this route – graceful trees of all colours, a mediaeval inn, hop gardens, rhododendrons and magnolias in full bloom.

Where the road runs along the crest of a ridge in the High Weald, views to both right and left stretch for miles. Already, although still in Sussex, the scenery was becoming rather Kentish with oast houses appearing here and there, many weatherboarded houses and a white-painted windmill. Drifts of forget-me-nots made a blue carpet; on the great chestnut trees spires of white flowers reached towards the sky.

Approaching the village of Burwash a signboard with the name Little Pook Hill was a reminder that we were now in Kipling country: in his Tudor house at Burwash (now a National Trust property) he wrote 'Puck of Pook's Hill' and many of his other stories or poems about Sussex. The village is attractive – here a Queen Anne doorway and bay windows, there a white façade smothered in wisteria, and everywhere gardens full of spring flow-

ers. To each side of the road as it continued onward were narrow lanes stretching downhill. Hawkhurst was yet another village with a big green, Georgian houses and an ancient church at the foot of a street leading uphill and past arcaded shops – to the coach station standing at the top among green fields, for a ten-minute stop.

On once more, through orchards now, to Rolvenden which, small though it is, has a museum of vintage cars run by the owner of one of the antique shops along its grass-edged streets. And still, wherever we went, the far views on both sides continued to be superb. Crab-apple trees were blossoming abundantly and ducks dabbled busily in lily pool and stream.

Tenterden, standing on a hill, can be seen long before one enters it. It is distinguished by the wide lawns which border its main road, and by the large number of Georgian houses that have survived the years unspoilt. Plenty of coaching inns here (the Caxton Inn has a particularly lovely cedar spreading its old branches wide just outside it), a half-timbered church and a town hall with its upper storey jutting over. The little town is a great place for markets: at one, you can buy anything from the freshest of fish or Shetland sweaters; for paintings go to the open-air art market held on the huge green; and there is a cattle market too. Those who linger here can find a figure-of-eight footpath well worth following around the old mill-ponds; and there is the old steam railway (with museum) for a scenic ride to Bodiam. In autumn, the copper beeches are a blaze of colour. (Stay or eat at the White Lion.)

After a while, the architectural styles began to change a little. There were quite a number of decorative Dutch-style gables, introduced by the Flemish refugees who fled to Kent after religious persecution in the Netherlands. From high coach windows I could see over hedges to the huge barns needed to house the abundance of this area and a paddock of grazing Arab horses. Some fields were brilliant with yellow oil-seed rape.

In and out of bustling Ashford, and then onward to Wye, an attractive spot surrounded by hop fields and the Wye Downs – beautiful hills owned by the National Trust. (Anyone stopping here for a while could go over the level-crossing and past a weir to explore this little Georgian town, its church and green. Wye Agricultural College has occasional open days and the gardens of Withersden Hall can sometimes be visited. Wye has several celebrated restaurants, and a good tea house.)

The road onwards repeatedly crossed the tranquil waters of the winding River Stour, before road and river apparently reach agreement to run harmoniously side by side. The green fields were at their brilliant best, woodlands at their freshest. Going downhill with trees arching overhead, it felt as if we were diving into a tunnel of green water. As we neared Canterbury, the Stour widened; the traffic began to increase; and we whirled over the top of the busy bypass carrying a procession of continental juggernauts from Dover to London.

We entered Canterbury via seedy outskirts (the terraced cottages were built for soldiers' families, during the days when the city was a military centre) and a modern roundabout, before sighting ahead of us the great Norman walls which still survive to enclose the ancient heart of the city. We followed them round, with a glimpse of Dane John (the great grassy hillock which is a prehistoric burial mound) as we went by, to come to a halt just within the east entrance, the one used for centuries by travellers from the continent and Dover.

The Coming of St Augustine

Stone Age people lived here; and Celts built a fort near the spot used later by the Normans for their castle. But it was the Romans who created the city, constructed its first walls and houses (the mosaic floor of one can be seen in Longmarket, near the coach station), and, in their last centuries here, built the first Christian churches. These fell into decay during the Saxon period but when, in 597, Augustine was sent by the Pope to re-Christianise England, he restored a number of them.

So, to start Canterbury's story from the beginning, I did not head immediately for the nearby cathedral but went first to St Martin's Church (a ½-mile walk along Longport, or take a bus), which was originally Roman – and some Roman bricks can be seen, re-used, in its walls. It is the oldest church in England still in use.

It was here that Bertha, Christian wife of the Saxon King Ethelbert (a pagan), used to pray – and here she provided Augustine and his monks with their first sanctuary. Only after King Ethelbert was converted were they able to build and preach freely elsewhere. Standing in the chancel of this modest little church perched on a hillside, I was standing where Saint Augustine had himself prayed; and it was at the stone font, with its Saxon-style decorations, that Augustine most probably baptised Ethelbert.

Outside, I wandered up among the old tombstones, wood anemones and yews to a terrace from which there are fine views – of the abbey which Augustine then founded (in 602), and beyond it the later cathedral (begun in Norman times).

To reach the abbey ruins, I retraced my footsteps along Longport: on one side, pink and green almshouses built in 1657 as a thank-offering for the birth of a baby to a couple who had been childless for twenty years, and on the other the prison, railed in with Roman fasces of cast iron. I went through the pretty garden that has been created around a Roman burial mound, now colourful with heather, the top of which provides a good view of the city. Beyond this is the abbey – in its time, a university long before Oxford or Cambridge.

It was – of course – Henry VIII who in 1538 reduced this to ruins (all except the 14th-century guest hall, which he and later monarchs found a useful lodging when travelling through Kent – it now belongs to King's School, so named when Henry took this, too, out of monastic hands). Among the towering, broken arches and the remnants of great stone walls are the tombs of Saxon kings and queens and of the very first archbishops of Canterbury, including Augustine himself, which survived successive rebuildings of the abbey throughout the middle ages. This vast complex of buildings, and its significance in English history, place the abbey ruins among the most important in Europe; and the site has a powerful presence.

Leaving the quiet ruins and their lawns for Monastery Street (with the glorious 13th-century Fyndon Gateway to the abbey still intact), I threaded my way through narrow streets towards the cathedral. There was plenty to look at on the way: I lingered outside the house of James Chilton, whose daughter was the first of the *Mayflower* pilgrims to set foot on American soil; at the bay-windowed shops which, for nine centuries, have been leaning at a tipsy angle over the road; and by the flint-and-ragstone church of St Paul, parts of which go back to Saxon times. I emerged to face the city wall and one of the few great bastions to have survived from the twenty-one originally built to defend the city.

Within the Walled City

In the Middle Ages it was Sandwich not Dover which was the principal port for travel to and from Europe; and pilgrims coming via Sandwich would have entered the city, as I now did, along the ancient road of Burgate (its name means 'the way in to the borough'). By contrast with the holy places of Canterbury, this is a quarter dedicated to commerce.

Bombing in the Second World War devastated much of Canterbury, so Burgate is a mixture. It's a street of small shops and cafés (much of it pedestrianised). There are still some old premises with panelled doorways or carved grotesques and foliage. One has a plaque to Thomas Barham and his poem about the cathedral's ghost, Nell Cook. Barham, Kentish poet-parson and author of 'The Jackdaw of Rheims', lived here. There's a National Trust shop; a Catholic church with a mural of all Canterbury's saints and early archbishops (and relics of Thomas Becket); and, by the 14th-century tower which is all of St Mary Magdalene's church that survived the bombs, a small garden in which to rest before pressing on. Even the modern stretches of Burgate are interesting – from decorative paving to the maple-leaf motif in balconies above a new parade of shops (a gift from Canadians, in memory of a Canadian killed by the bomb that fell here). Longmarket, to the left, has trees and seats among the shops: it is here that open-air carols are sung, with mayor and archbishop leading them, every December. Up Butchery Lane many mediaeval buildings survive (and a bull's head above what had for centuries been the butcher's shop – it closed only five years ago). Many of the older restaurants or inns in Burgate are known to have been pilgrims' hostels originally: Chaucers' pilgrims stayed at The Chequers of the Hope.

Burgate ends with what was once a bull-ring and before that a buttermarket. Behind its façades of Georgian plaster or imitation brick (actually 'mathematical tiles') lie mediaeval timbers and below are mediaeval wine vaults: you can visit one under Debenham's shop, as it is now a buttery.

Continuing past the great gateway that leads into the Cathedral precincts, I walked onwards up Palace Street (named for the archbishop's palace which was built on the right-hand side: another street of mainly 16th- and 17th-century houses and inns). On the corner of Sun Street, high up, is a scarlet pump marking the site of a spring from which flowed red water – reddened by Becket's blood, said the superstitious.

At the Mayflower Inn (a café now) some of the Pilgrim Fathers stayed in 1601 and here signed the agreement to charter the *Mayflower*. Between the houses there are arches through which coaches used to enter, and narrow alleyways (like flowery Turn-again Lane). The Priest's House, at no. 8, is decorated with big-breasted creatures that have cloven hoofs, carved and painted. All the way along, there are interesting architectural details: lozenge panes, decorative tile-hanging and pretty gables.

Opposite the big flint building which was part of the archbishops' palace (now used by King's School) is Conquest House, at no. 17, now a shop. This part-Saxon and part-Norman building was once an inn; and here the four knights who murdered Becket stayed on the night before the assassination. Their intention had been to murder him in the palace but when he fled for sanctuary to the cathedral they pursued him even there, the ultimate sacrilege. Over a fireplace is a painted coat-of-arms identical with one in the palace. The story goes that the artist engaged by the palace could not pay his inn bill and so discharged his debt by painting this replica.

No. 23 (now, like many others here, an antiques shop) was once the workshop of refugee Flemish weavers; and the Jacobean corner house – which tilts even more than the tower of Pisa – was a sweet shop selling humbugs and 'lemon stunners' to the King's School boys. Here, where the city walls curve round, used to be the north gate of Canterbury; and just beyond lie St John's Almshouses, their half-timbered gatehouse, gardens and Norman remains well worth visiting – the very first almshouses built in England, and still serving the same purpose today.

To get to another of Canterbury's main historical thoroughfares (St Peter's Street) I walked along backstreets. Canterbury's Benedictine monastery was, like all the greatest ones, a commercial powerhouse in Norman times, and for finance it often depended upon Jewish moneylenders – who congregated here, around the King Street area (where there is still an old synagogue, with lotus-topped pillars). So close was the relationship that some 7-branch candlesticks and vestments in Jewish style were used in the cathedral.

My walk took me past the remains of the Black Friars' monastery and down Best Lane, where a recently discovered well and clay pipes from Canterbury's pipe factory can be seen in front of the Kingsbridge Well restaurant. Opposite is a tiny garden in which to rest a while.

Pilgrims, Weavers and Friars

In St Peter's Street itself are the 12th-century hostel for poor pilgrims (spanning the River Stour), the 16th-century weavers' house (above the shop, you can watch a weaver at work there, or do brass-rubbings), the old ducking-stool for scolds behind it, boats for hire (or boat trips), and 15th-century Queen Elizabeth House (a restaurant). It was in this half-timbered house with elaborate plastered ceilings and gilded bosses that Elizabeth I finally told her suitor, the Duc d'Alençon, that she would have none of him. The great museum, its porch writhing with carved griffins, is mock-mediaeval: apart from its own displays of local and military history, its visiting exhibitions are of a very high standard – for instance, Degas sculptures when I was there. But St Peter's Street does not reveal all at a glance – below there are cellars to visit where Canterbury had its own mint, and above one can see the big top-storey doors through which bales of wool were hauled, to be spun and woven on the first floor, for sale on the ground floor (where the weaver's family would have had living quarters too).

The Poor Priests' Hospital and the remains of the Grey Friars' monastery take some finding, but are well worth it. I turned out of St Peter's Street to walk down Stour Street until I saw an archway with a nurseryman's sign on it. Through here lie 13th-century ruins, their grounds now used for growing plants. As I crossed the footbridge over the Stour (shallow, with brown trout, and green weed wavering in the current – 'stour' means fast-flowing; and ducks nesting on the bank), I could see the 14th-century bridge downstream – the earliest example of a brick bridge in England, the bricks being an innovation brought by Flemish refugees. A flowery path led to a quiet, sunny seat for a picnic beside the ruins and the mill-race. I could see the Franciscan monks' kitchen built across the river, with a trapdoor through which they could fish. Beyond the rows of plants was the Poor Priests' Hospital (part 12th-century and part Tudor; with café) and in the other direction the cathedral tower loomed above the rooftops. I knew that further along Stour Street is ancient St Mildred's church (more gardens) and the shell of the Norman castle in its green setting; but no place could be more attractive than Greyfriars for a restful hour – except perhaps West Gate Gardens. The West Gate is the only city gateway still standing (a small museum inside, and a fine view from its towers). The Stour, which is as tangled as a skein of wool, runs here too and on its banks a particularly pretty flower garden has been laid out: another of Canterbury's peaceful retreats from crowded streets.

Becket's Cathedral

What can I possibly write about the cathedral within the space of a few paragraphs? I have visited nearly every cathedral in England yet still this remains my favourite – not only for its beauty but because so much history has happened here. It is, too, one of the warmest and most colourful of cathedrals. I have returned again and again, for there is no way in which a single visit of, say, an hour or two can be sufficient.

So I will write about one thing only: the Becket story. The earliest parts of the present building date from 1070 (a previous structure had been destroyed by fire) and so it was exactly a century old when Archbishop Becket, having persistently defied Henry II's authority, was murdered by four knights. Immediately, the martyr became the centre of a cult, with all the paraphernalia of shrine, miracles, pilgrimages and so forth. Kent is full of churches dedicated to him.

Another fire gave the opportunity for fresh rebuilding (though the site of the assassination survived), on a splendid scale, to house Becket's jewelled tomb – until Henry VIII made off with its treasures and erased every trace of Becket that he could.

Later the Puritans did away with many other tombs, statues and stained glass; but despite this vandalism Canterbury's remaining mediaeval glass is some of the most outstanding in the world. The windows tell stories, in 'strip cartoon' form, for congregations that could not read, and among them is a long series of 13th-century windows relating the story of Becket's martyrdom, and of miraculous cures subsequently performed at his shrine (one window gives pilgrims a broad hint: a supplicant is shown handing over a bag of gold to one of the priests before praying at the shrine).

The Becket windows were designed half a century after the assassination, and the clothing is therefore in the fashion of that period (the time of King John). To understand every incident – and, indeed, all the cathedral's windows – it is well worth buying the little 'Guide to the Stained Glass' sold along with other excellent booklets (some for children) at the cathedral's bookstall. With its help one can pick out the crippled, the paralysed and the mad; those with toothache or epilepsy, recurrent nightmares or leprosy, swollen feet or the plague. All the miracle cures are shown in 'before' and 'after' pictures. But even more vivid testimony to the tremendous following that Becket's memory inspired are the dull stones beside the spot where his shrine stood, worn into hollows by the knees of the thousands who prayed there: recently, the Pope himself.

This is a tremendous cathedral, its nave soaring 80 feet high, filled with monuments to the great and the good (or not so good).

Even its Norman crypt is unique – the biggest in the world: a huge area skilfully covered with vaulting, some of its walls still painted with pictures from the same period. The delicate fan-vaulting below the tower, the elaborately carved effigy of the Black Prince lying on his tomb, the lovely cloisters, 'Bell Harry' tower (from which curfew is rung each night, the signal to close the gates of the precincts): any one of these would make Canterbury Cathedral worth a visit, and it has them all.

The 230-foot tower is a masterpiece. Despite its skin of stone, it was built from bricks – an almost unique achievement in 1498. Tremendously impressive at any time, it leaves an unforgettable impression if seen on a summer evening (or at Easter or Christmas) when it is floodlit: a grand finale to any visit to Canterbury.

SOME MORE PLACES TO VISIT For bus times and a free bus guide with map, tel. 0227 66151. As the following list shows, all round Canterbury are pretty villages in very lovely landscape, most having a church, green, old inns, stream, historic houses, picnic spots and footpaths. Fuller notes on them are in a free leaflet, 'Discover the Villages of Canterbury', obtainable from the Tourist Information Centre. The Centre also has the AA's Orchards Trail which, though designed for motorists, shows May blossom routes which buses, too, follow.

+**Blean** (buses no. 604–7, 684–7). Bird garden (exotic species). Café. Forest walks.

+**Bridge and Barham** (buses no. 615, 616 and, for Barham, 617). Fast road, but scenic. Two pretty villages, with good walks and views. One can alight from no. 615 or 616 at Barham crossroads and walk down past village green etc. to pick up no. 617 back.

+**Chartham Downs** (buses no. 651–3). Scenic ride. Walks on the Downs. Lunch at the Granville inn, Street End. Can walk back to Canterbury by the river (3 miles).

+**Chilham** (buses no. 400, 667, 668, all with short walk). Castle (with attractions such as falconry and jousting). Village of half-timbered houses. Scenic route – view of river, watermill, fields. Many cafés and inns.

+**Dargate** (bus no. 638). A winding apple-blossom route in May. Continues to Hernhill, on a hill, with green for picnicking; and Boughton – half-timbered houses, and good food at the White Horse.

Fordwich (buses no. 604–8, 684–7). ½ mile walk to village with historic houses, stocks, courthouse, river. Lunch at the George & Dragon. This was once Canterbury's port.

+**Harbledown** (buses no. 603, 333). Poor Priests' Hospital, friary ruins, etc. Main road, but scenic: orchards, far views. One can return by footpath to Canterbury's West Gate Gardens.

+**Littlebourne** (buses no. 612–14, 622). Alight at the Anchor inn. Village with oasts, Georgian houses, river, watermill, cricket field, and an attractive small green off the main road.

+**Patrixbourne** (buses no. 621 twice weekly; or, with 1½ mile walk, 615, 616,

617). Particularly lovely village: carved woodwork, stream, particularly interesting church, oasts, cricket field behind village for picnicking.

+**University of Kent** (buses no. 624, 625, 650). Fine views of Canterbury from hilltop campus. Excellent Gulbenkian Theatre.

Most of the above can be visited nearly every day of the year, but the following close in winter: Blean Bird Garden, Chilham Castle. For boat trips tel. 0227 62329.

SOME ANNUAL EVENTS May Mayor-Making (everyone wears lily-of-the-valley). **June** Rolls-Royce rally. Run Round City. **July** King's Week (music, drama). Folk Festival. Beer Festival. **Aug.** Cricket Week. Carnival. **Sept.** Hop Queen blessed in cathedral; Morris-dancing. **Dec.** Carol and other Christmas services in cathedral. Open-air carols with Mayor. Special services on Thomas Becket's Day (29th).

TOURIST INFORMATION CENTRE
22 St Peter's Street (0227 66567)
    Publications obtainable from the Centre include: See Canterbury in a Day (50p – excellent 40-page illustrated booklet); street plan (free); City of Canterbury guidebook that includes Whitstable, Herne Bay, etc. too (25p); Pilgrims Guide, historical (60p); quarterly events guide to east Kent, arts events and Gulbenkian Theatre programme (all free); Museums in Canterbury together with a trail from the coach park, which is also indicated by pavement arrows (free). There are various other city trails, overpriced at 50p; lots of booklets of country walks, and one on riverside walks in Canterbury (50p). Also regional information sheets (5p each) on special aspects of Kent – crafts, mills, Dickens, American connections, etc. Streets and Buildings shows the lesser-known byways in fine drawings (15p). Canterbury for the Disabled (50p); Information sheets on the city's

history, castle, Thomas More, etc. (free); Tourist and Leisure Scene (free). The Centre has times of guided town walks in summer; guided tours of the cathedral; and details of cycle hire. For a private guide, tel. 0227 65537.

ECONOMY TIPS Accommodation Youth Hostel: 54 New Dover Road. **Transport** Return fares on buses are cheaper after 9 a.m. and at weekends. Busrangers give a day's or week's unlimited travel in Kent and Sussex. Explorer tickets (see p. 206) are in course of preparation. **Admissions** Of the sights I have described, the following are free: city walls (there is a walk on top of part of them), Dane John, Norman castle, Poor Priests' Hospital – museum of Canterbury history opening in 1984, Royal Museum, Greyfriars, Weavers House, Conquest House, St John's Almshouses, East Bridge Hospital – a pilgrims' hostel. (It is cheaper to buy a combined ticket for the West Gate museum and the Roman pavement than to pay for each separately.)

EARLY-CLOSING DAY Thursday.

MARKET DAYS Cattle, Mondays. General, Wednesdays. Antiques and Crafts, Saturdays.

LOCAL ALE Canterbury ale and Shepherd Neame.

TO CHELTENHAM
from Heathrow Airport

Coaches depart approximately every 2 hours and the journey
takes about 2 hours. It goes through the rich agricultural areas
of Berkshire into the Cotswolds, with views of old stone
villages among the folds of the hills. Northleach is an interesting village at which to make a stop on the way.

It was a hot, hazy morning. The towers of Windsor Castle were just
a misty and romantic outline glimpsed briefly beyond the trees
before we turned off the M4 motorway to drive more slowly across
Farnham Common, knee-deep in summer grasses and tall buttercups. Oaks and plane trees stretched across this road, and the air
beneath their boughs smelt fresh after the fumes of the pounding
motorway.

Then, via a roundabout that was gay with marguerites and
clover, we joined another main route, the M40, and once more
gathered speed, flashing by overgrown hedges where elders were in
flower and, beyond these, the fields of wheat, grazing horses or
sheep with lambs. The windscreen became spattered with the
corpses of summer midges; and a steamy haze enveloped the far
hills which we saw intermittently between patches of old mixed
woodland or occasional conifer plantations.

Passengers dozed in the soporific heat. As the coach moved
faster, a welcome breeze poured in. There were occasional streams,
and a pool with a notice saying that carp and tench could be caught: I
envied the fish their cool depths. The road passed through a cutting,
chalk cliffs to either side, and emerged to a dramatic view of the
great plain ahead which we were now to cross. Here groups of cows
lay in the sparse shade of willows that traced the route of a stream,
while the sun beat down on the vacant grass.

We left the motorway for a shadier road fringed with spruce
and larch, then skirted Oxford to press on through an increasingly

attractive summer landscape. Meadows brimmed with wildflowers, and even the rushy streams were colourful with the flowers of waterweeds standing up above the surface. The lacey heads of cow parsley were like a great cloud of foam along miles of road. Already the fields of stiff and spikey barley were beginning to turn colour; there were scarlet poppies among the grain; and the lush green grass was being cut for silage.

We were now well into the Cotswolds and here, instead of hedges, drystone walls enclosed the fields – the honey-coloured blocks of limestone neatly laid, unlike the irregular stone walls of the Lake District. We were now high up and could see stone-built villages tucked away behind sheltering trees in the folds of hills, then the great spire of Burford's mediaeval church. Small cottages and great farms alike are made of the same beautiful Cotswold

stone, so readily worked into a variety of attractive details – shapely dripstones over mullioned windows, porches and steps, cornices and columns.

For some time we were stuck behind a long, slow lorry, heavy-laden with building materials. Eventually, even mild old ladies got impatient to overtake it but this was a winding road and 'better safe than sorry' said the patient driver. We passed slowly into Gloucestershire, grateful for the cool leaves of trees arching across the road before once again we were out among the fields. We went by the old stone Inn for All Seasons (one of the many small country hotels of excellence which I have described in my book *Staying Off The Beaten Track*) and at long last were able to pass the straining truck. Swiftly we drove by hedges of pink and white hawthorn with traveller's joy scrambling over them, a noble gateway leading to a distant mansion, flocks of bright white sheep (newly shorn), and donkeys dozing in a field full of meadowsweet – the scent drifted into the coach. Clusters of flowers hung down heavily from the sycamore trees.

The coach pulled up briefly at lovely Northleach, in which every mellow stone house is rooted in the past. There was a good view, while we paused, of the church's spectacular windows, and its immense tower. This is one of the most glorious examples of a church built entirely in the 15th-century Perpendicular style, at the height of the Gothic period. It was erected when Northleach was a wealthy centre of the wool trade – as were most of the houses one sees in the streets. Just outside Northleach, old stone farm buildings have been turned into the Cotswolds' own Museum of Rural Life.

There was not much further to go – up and down, with distant views to both left and right. The sign of the Puesdown Inn shows a stage coach stuck in the mire, with its passengers pushing it: probably a common enough incident on these hills when roads were little more than dirt tracks. We descended into the valley, fields of purple clover succeeded by a great manor house and the shining Dowdeswell reservoir with a solitary boatman and groves of pink rhododendrons right down to the water's edge. Here Cheltenham spreads itself out across the valley floor, and it took the coach a little while to get through the outskirts of Victorian villas behind privet hedges – a mixture, on this side of the town, of the seedy and the splendid. There were flying glimpses of one of Cheltenham's most elegant spots (Pittville Circus, with the entrance to Pittville Park close by – of which more later); of the birthplace of the composer Gustav Holst, now a museum; and of elegant terraces among green squares.

And then we had arrived, at one of the biggest coach stations in England, where sometimes as many as 300 coaches can be seen manoeuvring in and out. Its size is the reason why Cheltenham's coach station is (unlike most) not close to the town centre. So, finding it too sultry to face even a ten-minute walk, I taxi'ed to the centre of the Promenade where there is one of the few restaurants (the Black Tulip) able to provide on such a day a cool, uncrowded and quiet pause for lunch, before exploring Cheltenham further.

Regency Elegance

This is, par excellence, a town in which to stroll. It was laid out expressly for that purpose, and is on a level. Its pavements are wide, shaded by chestnuts planted in the Prince Regent's time, and plentifully supplied with seats. Lawns and flowerbeds are everywhere. And wherever you pause, there is something pleasurable or interesting at which to look: fountains, Regency architecture, elegant shops, sculpture, stucco or stone houses, lacey ironwork. It is one of the best of spa towns, created entirely because the fashionable world wanted to come and 'take the waters' when the excesses of London life had taken their toll, and to spend their summer in an atmosphere of elegance and recreation. Much of that original ambience still survives.

Further, Cheltenham being at the hub of a network of coaches (and buses), it is a good base from which to explore much of England.

The best starting point is the Tourist Information Centre (in the middle of the great Promenade, lined with sophisticated shops) where a 'walking tour' leaflet can be obtained, with notes about the architecture and history of the buildings in the Promenade; the famous Ladies' College; and – my favourite part – Montpellier Walk, with arcades of small shops, and dozens of caryatid figures copied from the Erecteum of Athens. (It is around here that many of the good guesthouses lie.) The Montpellier Gardens come at just the right moment for a rest, before tackling Suffolk Parade and the antique dealers' quarter. Little Trafalgar Street is worth seeking out, with the pretty cottage of Thomas Hardy's retirement years; and the colourful Imperial Gardens, yet another of Cheltenham's many green oases, a park with walled garden, beer tent in summer, fishpool and bandstand. At the Town Hall, you can help yourself to the famous alkaline waters (ugh!) from a blue Doulton urn in the foyer (it's here that most of the town's festivals and other big events are staged). Close by is Regent Street, the best place to look for a bistro-type meal (the food at the Everyman Theatre is good, too).

Leafy Suburbs

This perambulation of an hour or two covers most of Cheltenham's centre, the only part that most tourists bother to explore. But I have been back to the town a number of times, because there is so much more to discover. There is street upon street of handsome houses – terraced, or set back in their gardens, each with impeccable detailing in its balconies, classical pilasters, doorknocker, 'Gothick' porch, carefully proportioned lintels or frieze around the top – all best appreciated from the upper deck of a bus. There are ancient trees in the streets, and old 'piecrust' pillarboxes along the way.

For instance, a bus (no. 542) will take you to Pittville Park, through the town's most exclusive quarter (Pittville, named for Joseph Pitt who first developed it as a spa in 1825). Here are most of the very finest houses, and some excellent (yet not very expensive) hotels; and at their heart are 34 acres of informal parkland, flowers and lake with ducks, with the Pump Room. Children enjoy the aviaries and rabbit pens as well as the playground, and there is a nearby café. A boating lake and sportsground lies beyond – and a little further is Cheltenham's celebrated Gold Cup racecourse.

Sandford Park is more central. This has 14 acres with riverside paths, waterfalls, duck or fish pools, fountains, flowerbeds and an open-air swimming pool with café. (There are still more parks – the Tourist Information Centre has a leaflet with details about all of them.)

For anyone who wants to enjoy Cheltenham architecture away from the tourist-thronged hustle of the city centre, the no. 584 or 586 bus which heads down Park Place and returns via Lansdown Crescent gives a very good idea of the Cheltenham that only the residents know.

In complete contrast is the bus ride (no. 544 or 545) to the little village of Swindon, now almost a suburb of the town. This is where the huge recreation centre is, and a stadium (for squash, swimming, etc.). But Swindon is also a good starting point for country walks, described in a leaflet obtainable from the Tourist Information Centre.

There were two more things I wanted to see in Cheltenham – conveniently close to the coach station from which I would depart. One was the church with its tremendous 14th-century rose window, and the other was the museum and art gallery. This has acquired a magnificent new collection – a veritable treasure-house of *art nouveau* silver and metalwork, together with jewelry from the 18th-century to today (these are to go eventually to the Pump Room museum).

Cheltenham is the most complete of Regency towns. It is a garden-city, too, with trees and lawns everywhere. A town with every kind of shop or entertainment.

SOME MORE PLACES TO VISIT
Highly recommended: Cotswold Bus & Rail Guide (30p, from Tourist Information Centre), because this includes route map and timetables of even the smallest bus companies – and there are many of these, covering very lovely Cotswold countryside. It also contains street plans, suggested bus/rail and bus/walk outings, and much else of value to tourists. For bus information, tel. 0242 22021.
+**Bourton-on-the-Water** (bus no. P38).

Beautiful stream runs through centre of picturesque village. Free-flying parrots, etc. in bird gardens. Butterfly exhibition. Motor museum in water-mill. Perfumery. Model village and railway. (Also on this route: Upper Slaughter, with Tudor manor house.)
Broadway (buses no. C11, C15). The Cotswolds' showplace village. Antiques centre.
+**Cirencester** (buses no. 561, 562). Cathedral-like church, outstandingly good Roman museum, crafts centre,

market square, antique shops, inns.
+**Cleeve Hill** (bus no. C11). Spectacular views: 4-mile walk around Cleeve Common, with topograph at 1,085 feet up. Tourist Information Centre has leaflet about the walk. (Hailes Abbey is also on the C11 route.)
+**Coopers Hill** (bus no. 564). Fast road to hill with nature trail and views of woods. In May, there is a cheese-rolling race down its steep side.
+**Crickley Hill** (bus no. 563 to Air Balloon Inn). Country park, with nature trails, guided walks and remains of Iron Age camp.
Gloucester (buses no. 547, 548, 550 and – faster but less pretty routes – X25, 549, 559). Cathedral city in the Severn plain. Historic buildings, museum, shopping precincts, brass-rubbing centre, Beatrix Potter's *Tailor of Gloucester* in miniature scenes, etc. Leisure centre.
+**Leckhampton Hill** (buses no. 590, 591 plus steep walk). Fine views, fossils, wildflowers. 3-mile walk described in leaflet obtainable from Tourist Information Centre.
Miserden (buses no. 563, 918). Gardens open by appointment – tel. 309.
+**Overbury** (buses no. 539, 540). Pretty village on route through fields and orchards towards Vale of Evesham. Other pretty villages along the way are Kemerton and Alderton: houses of reddish stone here. Inn food.

Painswick (bus no. 564). Steep streets of ancient houses, fine church with notable tombs and 99 clipped yews, two centuries old. Art gallery. Inns. Palladian mansion.
+**Prinknash** (bus no. 564). Modern abbey: chapel, gardens and pottery open to visitors. Bird park, fish pools. Café.
Stanton (bus no. C11). Beauty-spot village of half-timbered houses, thatch, etc. Lunch at Mount Hill inn (steepish walk).
+**Stanway** (bus no. C11). Attractive rural ride. Inigo Jones gatehouse, church, etc.
+**Temple Guiting** (bus no. M40). Cotswold Farm Park: Britain's biggest collection of rare breeds. Playground, pets' corner, etc.
Tewkesbury (bus no. 542). Attractive route. Abbey, half-timbered houses, river trips (and launches to hire), riverside restaurants, old inns, museums. Silk mill.
Toddington (several services). Steam engine centre.
+**Winchcombe** (bus no. C11). Antique shops, inns, market square, houses of stone or half-timbered, railway museum. Sudeley Castle is ¾-mile walk (Catherine Parr's home; superb art treasures; historic toys; café; grounds for picnics).

Of the sights described above, the following are open on most days throughout the year: Tewkesbury Abbey, Prinknash bird park, Beatrix Potter museum, Corinium museum at Cirencester.

SOME ANNUAL EVENTS March Hobbies Exhibition. Cheltenham Gold Cup. **May** Antiques Fair. Competitive Festival of Music, Drama, etc. **June** Open-Air Art Exhibition. Ideal Home Show. **July** Music Festival. Horse Show. **Aug.** County cricket. **Sept.** Antiques Fair. Flower Show. Carnival. **Oct.** Literature Festival. **Dec.** Christmas Lights Festival.

TOURIST INFORMATION CENTRE Municipal Offices, The Promenade (0242 22878)
Publications obtainable from the Centre include: Cheltenham Spa Guidebook, with street plan (70p); mini-guide, with street plan (10p); lists of places to visit in vicinity, coaching inns, where to eat, events, antiques and book

shops, accommodation, cycle tours; Crickley Hill County Park trails (three, 10p each); Hill Walks around Cheltenham (70p); Town trail (free).

The Centre has details of guided walks, coach excursions and cycle hire.

ECONOMY TIPS Accommodation Youth Hostel: Cleeve Hill. **Transport** Rovercard, unlimited travel in and around Cheltenham. Day-Return, 25% saving at off-peak hours. Day-Out, unlimited travel throughout Bristol Omnibus region (from Evesham in the north down to Somerset, and east into Wiltshire). Children's Weekend Special, two children travel free if with two adults (on bank holidays too). **Admissions** Of the places I have described, the following are free: The museums and galleries (Cheltenham and Gloucester), Pittville Pump Room, Perfumery (Bourton), Cheltenham College, Silk Mill (Tewkesbury).

EARLY-CLOSING DAY Wednesday.

MARKET DAYS Street Market, Thursdays. Indoor Market, Tuesday to Saturday. Secondhand market at the Arts Centre, Saturdays. Craft Market, Saturdays.

LOCAL ALE & FOOD Donnington's ale. Double Gloucester cheese.

TO KING'S LYNN

from London

Coaches depart twice a day and the journey takes 3¾ hours from Victoria. It goes through rich farming country and wide heaths, across winding rivers and among forests.

It takes more than half an hour to get through the drearier parts of east London. After that, the route is a fast one, with the coach often achieving 70 m.p.h. as we flashed through a predominantly agricultural landscape, hurrying past occasional weatherboarded or whitewashed villages seen among the fields. The crops of rape (grown for the oil-rich seeds) were in their full blaze of colour, the sun streaming down on them: vast sheets of vivid yellow that were more dramatic even than daffodil fields. This is a gently rolling landscape in which church towers occasionally peep over the rounded hilltops, or sometimes an angler is glimpsed sitting patiently beside a lake where ducks are more actively engaged. Though the road runs straight, it undulates gently – sometimes running between embankments cut in the hills, sometimes emerging into woodlands or between fields. Near Newmarket a colourful group of jockeys were out exercising their horses.

Just over the Cambridge border, the coach paused at a café for a quarter-hour refreshment break and then we pressed on again. A chalk quarry with limeworks was succeeded by the rambling Bull Inn, its brick and whitewash half smothered in creeper. The scenery became more interesting as heath, Forestry Commission plantations, river, woods and fields alternated with one another. RAF Lakenheath is a big airfield that seemed to go on for mile after mile, the US and RAF flags flying side-by-side among the dozens of hangars, army trucks and camouflaged aircraft. A golf course followed, then still more wild heath.

Brandon is an attractive little town, neat with rows of pollarded limes and flint-walled houses. While the coach paused to pick up passengers, I passed the time spotting the seemingly infinite variety of ways in which flints had been used to decorate the walls (one of the local pubs is called The Flint Knapper). The beautiful Little Ouse winds its way through Brandon, lawns sloping down to the waters where small boats moor. Several pleasant hotels cluster here, before the level-crossing and the onward road through Breckland, the land of 'breaks' – meaning heathland intermittently cultivated over thousands of years by prehistoric tribes who found the soil and the streams well suited to their needs. A signpost points to Grimes Graves, a mile to the right – not graves but a network of Stone Age flint mines dug deep into the chalk ten thousand years ago. There are hundreds of them, some open to visitors, and some still with flint tools abandoned by their makers.

The road here is lined for many miles with pine trees which over the years have been twisted by the wind into convoluted shapes

– like Japanese bonsai writ large. The conifers of Thetford Forest followed; and more signposts that are a reminder of the area's prehistoric past – at Cockley Cley, for instance, a Celtic village has been reconstructed.

Swaffham is another pleasant, small town of flint and brick, predominantly Georgian. It was market day: stalls thronged the main street and surrounded the little cupola with Ceres, goddess of plenty, perched on top. More fields of rape and more water towers (the eastern side of England is chronically short of rain), and then came the big watermill, trout farm and restaurant at Narborough. The architecture began to change: instead of flint or brick walls, more and more buildings were made of the rough, orangey-red carr stone peculiar to the north of Norfolk. This was a sign that King's Lynn was near, and within minutes we had arrived at the coach station – conveniently central, as usual, and right by the town museum (which is always a good thing to visit first in order to understand the natural and the man-made history of what one is going to see thereafter).

Waterside Origins

The town began as a string of houses along the edge of the then winding River Ouse, there conducting so prosperous a trade with northern Europe that Lynn became England's fourth greatest port for a while. The big river, which provided a main route into the Midlands, was straightened and widened in Victorian times, but its original course is still indicated by the winding line of the town's most historic thoroughfare, built up in stages and now known as Nelson Street, Queen Street and King Street.

Along here are to be found buildings that go back to the time of the Norman bishops who founded and controlled Lynn; and a walk from one end to the other (terminating in the big Tuesday Market Place) will cover much of what is most interesting in Lynn. To get from the coach station to the start of such a walk, one passes the old Greyfriars Tower – last remnant of a big monastery (retained as a landmark for seamen), surrounded by a little garden where I was tempted to linger. This was just one of many monasteries that flourished here. The tower marks the edge of the old town: everything eastward was built centuries later.

Nelson Street starts at the little creek known as Millfleet, frequented by a flock of over a hundred swans. From a seat by the waterside, one can see the backs of the old maltings (sensitively converted to flats), moored boats and the tall chimney of what was once a cattlefood mill – now used for budding steeplejacks to practise on. Nearby in Bridge Street is a fine 17th-century house once known as the Greenland Fishery Inn because it became the headquarters of the whaling fleet. Along Nelson Street itself is another of Lynn's treasures, Hampton Court. Through a wide arch with little heads is a cobbled court surrounded by a mixture of buildings: 15th-century shops at the front, the warehouse of a merchant on what was the river frontage. Hampton Court stands by the junction of four ancient lanes, and it is worth risking life and limb to stand in the middle of the roadway here to look down each in turn – very little changed since the Middle Ages. Some of the timbered houses, with their upper stories jetted over the road, have attractive herringbone brickwork.

A few yards down one of them, Priory Lane, I wandered through a great archway (only recently unblocked) to find myself in a peaceful court of cobbles and flowers with a well at the end, and ancient buildings around it – once a priory – that have been restored for use as homes: beautifully done, the scheme deservedly won a conservation award. Along Lynn's old streets, there are many such arches with gardens beyond; small alleyways; and decorative touches like the pelicans that are the town's symbol carved above doorways or cast in iron as weathervanes.

A fortress-like building further along is a Hanseatic warehouse (the Hansa was a 15th-century league of German merchants to whom the king had sold trading privileges: not surprisingly, English traders were hostile to them and they built accordingly). Part of it became St Margaret's House: although the fine house with Georgian façade is now offices, one is free to walk in and I paused briefly to sit among the sunny flowerbeds in its cobbled yard. There are millstones laid out here: once, Lynn did a busy trade importing these essentials of life before the Industrial Revolution. Next to it is the house where Fanny Burney grew up.

The Treasures of an Ancient Church

A flower-bordered path leads to the door of St Margaret's church. On a unique and colourful dial above, the phases of the moon and the times of high tides are recorded – the ingenious work of a 17th-century churchwarden – and tidemarks by the door indicate the importance of such information in the life of Lynn: as recently as January 1978 the town was inundated by a freak tide, with 4 feet of water flooding into the church.

St Margaret's is a church of very great splendour, built by monks in the centuries of Lynn's greatest prosperity. A little Norman work remains, but some of its most decorative features are from the 14th century – the fine carving of the screens, for example, and two of the church's most famous treasures, a pair of huge brasses (probably of Flemish workmanship) which are the biggest in Britain. Here lies the portrait of a former mayor of Lynn with his first and second wives at either side, and along the foot a frieze depicting a banquet of considerable splendour – it's worth kneeling to study all the tiny details: bearers of roast peacocks, musicians, even the goblets and knives on the table, and the fashionably pointed shoes of the diners. On another brass, an everyday story of country life is the theme: there is a post-mill and (an allusion to a folk tale) a man carrying corn to relieve his tired horse.

Nearly every century has left its own distinctive touch on the church. The pulpit with its marquetry panels is Georgian, so is the organ which was made to the design of Fanny Burney's father when he was organist here. The aluminium altar that stands before the chancel is uncompromisingly of our own time, set within a grey brick surround of unusual shape.

Lynn's church has problems (all too evident when I looked at the startling angle of the arches under the great tower). The banks of the Ouse were marshy and repeatedly subsidence below and gales or flood-tides above have done their worst. One of the ways in which money is raised for repairs is by serving refreshments on market days, within the church itself.

Through Streets Broad and Narrow

Just outside the church is the Saturday Market Place with the distinctive 15th-century Town Hall built of stone and flint in chequerboard style (the Tourist Information Centre is here). When I visited it, changes were afoot but even in disarray it was a building worth exploring – the sun poured in through great windows with views of the church, stone-flagged floors and ancient oak doors were succeeded by Georgian assembly rooms of faded elegance, all gilt and portraits, and the now deserted formalities of the old courtroom. In an undercroft adjoining this building the town's regalia is exhibited, including a famous gilt cup (pint-size) of 1325, elaborately decorated with courtly figures, called King John's Cup.

To continue the walk, along narrow Queen Street, is a hairraising experience, for big lorries thunder along this stretch with little regard for pedestrians on the scant pavements. Under these conditions, I gave the 18th-century barley-sugar columns of Clifton House only a quick glance (although the mediaeval interior is open to visitors, and its watchtower too), and was glad to walk a few yards back and find a quieter refuge behind a carved oak door, in the courtyard garden of 15th-century Thoresby College (which now combines a youth hostel and flatlets for old people). The seats among the lawns and shrubs were welcome at this point. One can go out on the far side to stroll along the South Quay (paved with setts). The tide was out and I could see the great build-up of mud which is such a problem in the Ouse: an incoming tide takes only 3 hours, but the ebb is slow (9 hours) which means colossal quantities of silt are deposited. A cargo ship was loading grain, and there was a fine view out to The Wash. A little further along, craftsmen were at work on jewelry and pottery in an old granary (in King Staithe Lane).

Back, then, to the streets. At Purfleet creek, where the classical little Custom House stands with a cupola on top and a grandiloquent statue of Charles II above the door, King Street takes over – rather wider and mostly of more recent date than Queen

Street. Although the fronts are Georgian, I could see in the alleys between them the half-timbering and old barns which date the houses as being much earlier. Nos. 28–32 are of particular interest: very recently a huge Norman stone hall was discovered hidden in the heart of a more recent structure. Only some considerable magnate could have had such a home in those days. Accretions have now been stripped away and soon the house may be open to the public, as a heritage centre. Along here there are some of the very earliest brick buildings, too. Lynn, having no stone at hand, began early on to use clay for brick-making, a technique learnt from the Dutch with whom they traded (which is why some buildings in this region have gables in the Dutch style).

The further I walked, the more interesting the street became. The town's museum of social history is here (a graceful building – the hall has fluted pillars and an oval fanlight above). It contains old kitchens, dolls and domestic trifles (a brass-rubbing centre, too); and next door is the hall of one of the 26 trade guilds which flourished in King's Lynn, now owned by the National Trust. It is the largest 15th-century guildhall in Britain. A complex of old, red-brick buildings houses an art gallery, a good restaurant with water-front view and terrace, and an intimate theatre, under the wood-pegged 15th-century rafters of which artistes like Janet Baker and Kathleen Ferrier can be heard much better, they say, than in the huge concert halls of London.

The Tuesday Market

This is the great set-piece of the town. Back in the 12th century, the citizens of Lynn (which was in those days Bishop's Lynn and not King's Lynn) got their first charter to hold a market, from the bishop. Such a charter meant a lot to a town for it then received rents from the stallholders.

Lynn's Tuesday Market grew bigger and bigger. Hence this enormous square, surrounded by its grandest buildings: magnates' houses of stone or brick, the Corn Exchange with a distinctly sexy corn-goddess on top, and the great coaching inns. But more than commerce took place here. Where the rows of parked cars are packed in, people died. Two children were hanged in 1708 for stealing. A witch was hanged, too – her heart, it was said, burst from her body and struck a nearby building: look closely on the north side and there on a red brick façade is an outline of a heart, on (the story goes) the very spot where the flying heart struck. And most gruesome of all was the death in 1531 of a maidservant who poisoned her mistress. For a short perod, boiling was a legal form of execution in England for this crime, and thus, lingeringly, she died.

I turned away from the outwardly gay square with some feeling of relief, to make one last visit. This was to the church in the fishermen's quarter, which is dedicated to the fishermen's patron, St Nicholas. It is a beauty, not to be missed – with a soaring angel roof and a multitude of fine monuments, some of marble, some gilded and painted. During the summer festival, the Queen Mother attends concerts here. The music starts as the dying sun pours in through the windows; daylight fades; and at the end the angels are illuminated.

Back in the Tuesday Market Place I had wondered at people who chose to eat their sandwiches on the steps of a bank, surrounded by cars. I wondered even more when, just a few minutes away, I found behind St Nicholas' church (where old and new fishermen's cottages huddle together) a small garden and seat, providing a tranquil spot in which to end a town walk.

SOME MORE PLACES TO VISIT For bus times and free route map, tel. 0553 2343. Many routes eastward are through woodland or heath, and go to villages or market towns remarkable for very fine churches and for buildings of the local reddish carr stone. Every village has its own pictorial sign, carved and painted. Westward lie the flat fens, criss-crossed with streams and dykes.

Caley Mill (buses no. 410–13). Lavender farm of 100 acres, with riverside garden, café in the old watermill, rosebeds. Lavender is harvested in July/ August. In other months, there is an audiovisual show. Herbs for sale.

+**Castle Acre** (bus no. 437). Flint village around a long green, with fine priory ruins at far end and an exceptional church. Castle ruins on mound beyond the village. Lunch at the Ostrich inn.

+**Castle Rising** (buses no. 410–413). Norman castle on a mound; church; pretty village; and Black Horse inn for meals.

Dersingham (bus no. 411). Straggling village of old cottages, 17th-century barn, notable features in the church; with (a ½-mile walk) pottery and café.

+**Great Bircham** (bus no. 415). Alight at King's Head and walk along tracks to visit the old windmill (5 floors)

and bakehouse. Cycles (with route maps) can be hired at the mill.
+Great Massingham (bus no. 468). Village with green, two duckponds, well and fine views. Lunch at Rose & Crown.
Heacham (buses no. 410–413). An attractive ride in summer when fields of lavender are in flower. Lunch at The Wheatsheaf near church and village green. Sandy beach is ³⁄₄-mile walk.
+Houghton Hall (bus no. 468 to Harpley). A pretty route, then a 1-mile walk to the deer-park gates, ³⁄₄ mile more to the grandiose mansion (home of Britain's first prime minister, Walpole: state rooms, horses, 20,000 model soldiers, café).
+Hunstanton (410–13). Children love miles of golden sands, rock pools, amusements and seafront gardens. Boat trips. Clifftop walks. LTA Tennis Tournament. Regatta. Mini-guide obtainable from Tourist Information Centre.
+Sandringham Country Park (buses no. 410, 412, 413). Alight at Wolferton. Turn to walk through rhododendrons (glorious in June) to the country park (nature trails, guided walks and café). Return by bus no. 411.

Sandringham House (bus no. 411). The royal home, church and superb grounds. Flower show in July. Royal vintage cars. Pick your own apples in September, soft fruit earlier.
Swaffham (buses no. 434–8). Georgian town with lively market on Saturdays; antique shops; restaurants; church with angel roof and fine monuments. The route passes Narborough (watermill and trout farm).
Terrington St Clement (bus no. 505). African violet centre.
+West Newton (bus no. 411). Cottages belonging to the royal estate of Sandringham.
Wisbech (bus no. 336). The route skirts the Fens, and runs alongside the river Nene. Dutch-style riverside town. Peckover House (National Trust): Georgian town house, garden, etc. (café). Museum. Markets on Thursdays and Saturdays. Rose fair in July.
Wolferton (buses no. 410, 412, 413). A lovely woodland ride with rhododendrons flowering in June leading to village and the station once used by royalty, now a museum with items from royal trains.

Most of the above can be visited nearly every day of the year, but the following close in winter: Merchant's House, Regalia Rooms, Sandringham Country Park, Wolferton Station Museum, Houghton Hall, Peckover House, Castle Acre Priory, Sandringham House (this also closes when the royal family stay there in midsummer).

SOME ANNUAL EVENTS Feb. Mart (fair). **March** Flea Market (also in June, Sept. and Dec.). **May** Mayoral procession. May Day Morris Dancers. **July** Arts Festival. Sandringham Flower Show.

TOURIST INFORMATION CENTRE
Town Hall, Queen Street (0553 63044)
    Publications obtainable from the Centre include: King's Lynn Mini-guide with street plan (free); King's Lynn Walkabout, produced by Eastern Counties bus company (free: an invaluable help to anyone who wants to start out and return to the coach station); West Norfolk – Lynn and environs, colourful booklet (free); West Norfolk Guide, describes all the villages and towns (free); list of eating places (free); Looking at Lynn – historical buildings (30p); information sheets on docks and on cattle market (free); Nature Re-

serves in Norfolk (free); King's Lynn guidebook (£1.80).

The Centre has times of guided walks, ferry over the Ouse, and coach excursions.

ECONOMY TIPS Accommodation Youth Hostel: Thoresby College. **Transport** Anywhere bus tickets allow you a day's unlimited travel on Eastern Counties buses. **Admissions** Of the sights I have described the following are free: parts of the Caley Mill Lavender farm, Sandringham Country Park, Fermoy art gallery, Custom House.

EARLY-CLOSING DAY Wednesday.

MARKET DAYS Tuesdays, Fridays (in the Tuesday Market Place; includes Womens Institutes' market), Saturdays. Cattle Market, Tuesdays.

LOCAL ALE & FOOD Greene King and Elgood's ales. Shrimps from The Wash. Pork haslet. Samphire.

TO LOWESTOFT

from Chelmsford

Coaches depart approximately 4 times a day and the journey takes about 3 hours. It goes through a serene countryside networked with rivers and streams, passing noble churches and historic market towns. There are several possible stops on the way, such as Ipswich (historic port and county town); Wood-bridge (Georgian town with old tide-mill at the head of the estuary); or Southwold (elegant old seaside resort).

There had been one of those abrupt summer cloudbursts in which rain bounces high off the pavements and cascades along the over-flowing gutters. But as we set off it stopped as suddenly as it had begun ten minutes earlier, and very clear light began to struggle through the gaps that were now widening between the grey clouds. We joined the main road along which so many coaches and lorries make their way from the east coast ports, the latter laden with great shipping containers from all over the world.

The road ran straight ahead, across a flat landscape. We crossed over the River Stour and thus into Suffolk, rather more hilly and with more trees than Essex. This is Constable country (sign-posts pointed to Flatford Mill), with occasional thatched cottages among the orchards and the corn.

The River Orwell and a canal were crossed, and soon we were in Ipswich – but with only fleeting glimpses of its historic buildings, half-timbered and pargetted, and of ancient church towers.

Once beyond the rambling suburbs of the town, it is no distance to Woodbridge: the coach accompanied the shining River Deben downstream, passed Notcutts attractively landscaped gar-den centre, and drew up in a narrow street of terraced cottages with Georgian and Victorian façades and demure porches against pink plaster walls (but some with jetted upper storeys suggesting a mediaeval structure behind).

As we moved on through the town, there was a momentary view of the estuary, a colourful picture of boats swaying in the water beyond banks sprinkled with red poppies and purple mallows. Past pillared mansions we went, and inns with window boxes of geraniums, and colourwashed houses with fretted gables. There were sedate gardens seen over the tops of mellow brick walls, cheerful cottage gardens, and businesslike nursery gardens. The coach paused in the centre of Wickham Market giving a few minutes in which to enjoy a scene of country shopping: the half-timbered greengrocery, the butcher's striped awning, white shutters and baskets of lobelias and geraniums outside another shop – and no chain stores, plate-glass or strident advertisements.

On once more, through fields of brown barley and dark green spinach, repeatedly crossing rivers or streams. Sometimes walls were made from flints but often the houses were of brick with pantiled roofs and shapely gables – the Dutch influence – or, typical of Suffolk, colourwashed and with well-proportioned sash windows. There was a watermill on one of the rivers, many barns (black-boarded walls and red roofs), and occasional mansions in parks set well back from the road.

The flint church of Saxmundham came into view across the fields before we passed through the town itself – typically East

Anglian, with plenty of antique shops and inns among Georgian houses draped with wistaria or creepers.

The fields grew steadily larger as the leafy road wandered on, gently up and down, passing thatched and whitewashed cottages and lodges of flint or of rustic-work. One field was a blazing sheet of poppies; in another strawberries glimmered within the cushions of leaves. Then, past a heath of sand dunes and gorse, came one of the most spectacular sights of the journey: Blythburgh's great church with its huge clerestories running all the way below each side of the roof, so that one can see right through them both and to the blue sky on the other side.

The agricultural landscape changed to marsh, river, and then sea views. Beyond banks of bracken, we could see into Gwatkin Nature Reserve – a place of reeds, streams, butterflies and birds. Even the verges of this stretch of road were an unofficial nature reserve, thronged with wildflowers: their names are enough to evoke an English summer – clover, briar roses, cow parsley, vetch, honeysuckle, buttercups, elderflowers, thistles.

Southwold has not one village green but a dozen, and we passed some on our way in and out. There was a close full of old-fashioned roses, and more than a few glass porches crammed to bursting with pot plants. The wrought-iron signs and striped awnings of the shops, a Victorian lamp-post with dolphins and hanging flower baskets, and rambler roses on sun-baked walls, all contributed to the discreet gaiety of the town. Many houses by the sea have glass verandahs, with canvas chairs facing the morning sunshine. Prince William had been born the previous day, so union flags were flying outside inns and the town hall.

We left the sea behind to follow winding country lanes that took us among oaks, across rivers bright with yellow water-lilies and past gardens of pansies, lupins and delphiniums. Suddenly busy Lowestoft had arrived. We entered it via streets of shabby Victorian guesthouses and ticky-tacky shops. Ahead, cranes and ships' masts showed where the harbour lay, but our route wound through backstreets not along the seafront, to reach the coach station just behind the main (pedestrianised) shopping street of the town.

Harbour, Beaches and Broads

Lowestoft, England's most easterly town, has a split personality. There is historic Lowestoft, of which – apart from the fishing quarter – only traces are left. Commercial Lowestoft, which dominates the centre, is a dehumanised mass of fish-freezing factories and fast one-way streets that are a nightmare to motorists and pedestrians alike. Seaside Lowestoft – the southern half – is a pleasant resort with miles of golden sands for a traditional holiday. To this list one can add inland Lowestoft, with Oulton Broad – a watery wilderness as popular as any of the Norfolk Broads. So you need to pick your way carefully in order to find the particular kind of Lowestoft that you want.

Fishing was and is at the heart of Lowestoft, so I chose to go first to the harbour (a short stroll back across the bascule bridge – where I had one of the cheapest lunches of my journey, in a comfortable and uncrowded restaurant out on the South Pier, with superb views whilst I ate: a good start). Through big windows, I could see several harbours frequented by kittiwakes; one is used by the Royal Norfolk and Suffolk Yacht Club, with every kind of craft from sportive catamarans to the homely fishing-boats of the long-shoremen, lifeboat and pilots' boats; another is for the trawlers. Angling trips set out from here. A huge oil tanker passed by – complete with cranes and helicopter pad – on its way to the North Sea oil rigs (sometimes one can see the massive parts of new rigs being towed out, huge structures as big as factories). Beyond lay the colourful buildings of the various vice-consuls' offices, the Fisher-men's Mission and the fish market. One has to book ahead (tel. 0502 65989) to be sure of a place in the very popular tours of this, to see fish being landed and filleted, the ice factory and the auctions; and to go on board one of the trawlers. Occasionally there is a chance to board a visiting warship, or to watch sea-rescue demonstrations. You can buy fish from one of the warehouses in Battery Green Road; at the kiosks of the longshoremen; or, as I did, from the historic smokehouse in Raglan Street (a listed building) where herrings are kippered in the proper, traditional way over slow-smouldering piles of oak chips.

The whole story of Lowestoft fishing is told in exhibits at the Maritime Museum near the north end of the seafront (best reached by buses no. 680 or 681, with glimpses along the way of the steep passageways known as The Scores) where you might, if lucky, be shown round by one of Lowestoft's characters – ex-skipper Vernil Tuck. It needs time to pore over the miscellany of treasures here – everything from traditional shipwrights' tools to a scale model of a modern oil rig, and poignant bits of wreckage such as the name-board of a trawler sunk by U-boats which came ashore 60 years later. There's an array of lifeboat models – and the marble trophy (given by Madame Prunier of fish restaurant fame) which went annually to the skipper who landed most herrings in one night: it is no longer awarded, for the days when some 50,000 were to be netted at a go have long past.

Outside, scarlet salvias blazed beside a smooth bowling-green overlooked by the old, white lighthouse on a bank above, and, in the adjoining suntrap gardens, preparations were in progress for an open-air concert. Here is a café, too, and the Sparrows' Nest – formerly the headquarters of the Naval Patrol Service, and now a museum full of mementoes from the time when heroism was a daily occurrence as the small patrol vessels went out to clear mines from the waters of the North Sea during the Second World War. Close by is pretty little Bellevue Park.

The beaches up at this end of Lowestoft are sandy, with dunes, and if you choose to walk further along you come to Gunton Cliffs, a good picnicking spot with paths wandering among the heather and other wildflowers – and, if you get up at dawn, a fine spot from which to see some of the most spectacular sunrises in England.

Most people prefer the sands to the south, however, where there are piers, hotels, bathing huts, traffic-free esplanade, gardens and all the usual amenities of a popular resort. Yet even though I was there on a hot, sunny day in June, I found the miles of golden beaches uncrowded. Plenty of cafés, of course, but you can eat even better (yet still at a modest price) if you head for the Buttery Bar of one of the grand hotels, the Victoria. Those visiting by coach for just a day by the sea would do best to pop onto a bus (no. 680, 681 and

682) for the few minutes' ride to Kensington Gardens, which stands just above the centre of the south beach. The Gardens have a Japanese-style rock garden, aviary, lake and café. This south front is where the children's narrow-gauge railway is, and the Punch & Judy show. Anyone choosing this coastline for a taste of the traditional seaside is likely to get plenty of sun, and little rain – but a windbreak is a rather necessary precaution.

As to Lowestoft's other main attraction, there are three ways to reach Oulton Broad: either by taking a leisurely riverside walk to it from Eastern Way, behind the railway station, or by rail, or by bus (no. 683).

The 1¼-mile walk is an attractive one, passing through the green acres of Normanston Park which has a wildfowl reserve (and a café) before arriving at the lock which separates the salty Lake Lothing, which is not really a lake but part of the River Waveney, from the fresh waters of Oulton Broad – acres of opportunity for boating or water sports (Thursday is the day for watching world-class powerboat racing there). If you do not want the entertainments (including free swimming pool) of the north end, in Nicholas Everitt Park, press on a little farther – to Oulton Broad South, where Marsh Road and a footpath lead to quieter banks from which to watch the sailing-boats go by.

SOME MORE PLACES TO VISIT For bus times and route map, tel. 0502 65406. Most routes go through pleasantly undulating Suffolk countryside: good walking country.

Beccles (buses no. 631, 671; or by boat on Fridays – market day – from Oulton Broad). Old buildings, quay with hundreds of small boats, large common, museum. Annual regatta. The route passes Barnby which has a 13th-century thatched church. Plenty of restaurants, such as the Loaves and Fishes by the river.

Carlton Colville (buses no. 631, 671, 681). East Anglia Transport Museum of vintage buses, cars, etc. Narrow-gauge railway and tram rides. A good restaurant at Hedley House Hotel.

+Covehithe (buses no. 601–610 alight at Wrentham). Mere, ruined church and crumbling cliffs.

Dip Farm (buses no. 601–610). Glades, and acres of grassland. Steam train, bumper boats, café, etc. Footpaths to sea. Lowestoft's nudist beach is near here.

+Earsham (bus no. 631). The Otter Trust: otters and wildfowl in natural surroundings. Café.

+Gorleston (buses no. 601–610). Short walk to sandy seafront. This resort, on a low cliff, faces Yarmouth's fish wharf across the mouth of the River Yare.

+**Hopton** (buses no. 601–610). Holiday villages and markets; cliffs and sands. The route passes Corton (interesting church, footpaths to beach).
+**Kessingland** (buses no. 601–610). Wildlife park: tigers, monkeys, macaws, etc. Narrow-gauge railway. Café. Miles of beach.
Lound (bus no. 637). Alight at the Village Maid inn, with Lound Manor bird farm (200 species) beside the village pond with swans; and walk back to 'the gold church': its gilded, carved interior makes many a cathedral look dowdy. The route goes through Blundeston with the Plough Inn of *David Copperfield*.
Lowestoft Leisure Centre (bus no. 688, 689). Swimming, squash, table tennis,

roller skating, gymnasium and many other sports, plus sauna and solarium. Café.
+**Oulton** (bus no. 688). Alight at Prospect Road which leads to a track called Boathouse Lane, and an unfrequented side of Oulton Broad. George Borrow lived here – his octagonal summerhouse still stands.
Wangford (buses no. 601–610). Splendid church, old cottages, lovely setting. Music festival in July. Eat at the Plough or the Suffolk Poacher.
Worlingham (buses no. 631, 671). The Hall opens to the public in June.
Yarmouth (buses no. 601–610). A ¾-hour ride, to 'the Blackpool of the east coast'.

Many of the places described can be visited on most days throughout the year, but the following close in winter: fish-market tours, Punch & Judy, Otter Trust, wildlife park and all the museums.

SOME ANNUAL EVENTS April Hockey and rugby festivals. **May** Oulton Broad regatta and fête. 'Petticoat Lane' street market. **June** Regatta. **July** Donkey Derby. **Aug.** Carnival and summer show. Junior tennis championship. Cricket Week. Sea Week. Oulton Broad regatta. **Sept.** Battle of Britain week (flying and power-boats). **Oct.** Sea-angling festival.

TOURIST INFORMATION CENTRE
The Esplanade (0502 65989)
Publications obtainable from the Centre include: Waveney guidebook with accommodation list (Waveney is the area that includes Lowestoft, Beccles, Southwold, etc.) (free); Lowestoft mini-guide with town plan (10p); Lowestoft Through the Ages (65p); Walks In and Around Waveney (25p); Lowestoft Then and Now – a trail through the older parts (35p); Lowestoft Nature Trails – Gunton, north beach,

Normanston Park and south beach are covered (rather pricey at 90p); footpath map of Oulton Broad district, and others (40p each).
The Centre has details of boat trips, boat and cycle hire, pleasure flights and coach excursions.

ECONOMY TIPS Accommodation Discounts for pensioners early and late in the season. **Transport** Anywhere tickets entitle the user to a day's unlimited bus travel in the area covered by Eastern Counties buses (virtually all of Suffolk and Norfolk). Ten Trip are ten tickets for the price of nine. The Suffolk Coastliner is a summer bus which travels from Yarmouth and Lowestoft all the way to Felixstowe and back in a day. Explorer tickets (see p. 206) cover journeys from Lowestoft to Southwold, Yarmouth, the Norfolk Broads, Norwich, Diss and the Waveney Valley: on some trips, free booklets or reduced admission fees to 'sights' are included. **Admissions** The piers and Lound Manor bird farm are free.

LOCAL ALE & FOOD Adnams. Fish of all kinds.

EARLY-CLOSING DAY Thursday.

TO NOTTINGHAM
from North London

Coaches depart from Golders Green approximately every
2 hours and the journey takes about 3½ hours (or, from
Victoria, 4 hours). There is a shorter route which takes three-
quarters of an hour less. The longer and more scenic way which
I chose goes through the valleys and sandstone villages of
Northamptonshire, a rich agricultural area with fine scenery,
known as 'the county of squires and spires', and with much
Civil War history to it. An interesting stop on the way would be
at Market Harborough, a traditional centre for hunts as well as
for markets (or else at the great cities of Northampton and
Leicester, although their few remaining buildings of interest,
and their various museums, are overwhelmed by monstrous
modern blocks).

Within minutes the coach had bounced through the suburbs to join
the cavalcade of lorries and cars that were pounding their way north
along the M1. Our driver kept to the fast lane, steadily overtaking
other traffic as we flashed by green fields and hawthorn hedges, our
speed sending a refreshing breeze in through the ventilators. This is
one of the least interesting motorways, until the north is reached,
but a very smooth one; and many passengers closed their eyes to
snooze their way through this part of the journey.

We passed into Bedfordshire: dozens of tall brickworks' chimneys on one side, trucks of bricks joining the traffic. There were
juggernauts bearing floor-coverings south from Lancaster, beer
from Yorkshire and shoes from Leicester. Containers proclaimed
their more distant origins – New Zealand, Finland, USA. Some
tankers were full of lager, some of cement. The M1 is one of the
great trade routes.

We turned aside to call at Northampton, passing a pub at
Hardingstone named after Eleanor, the beautiful queen of Edward
I, whose body remained overnight here on its long progress from

Lincolnshire to be buried in Westminster Abbey – the spot is marked by a decorative stone cross which the king placed here, as at a dozen resting places on the journey; and by a great field being prepared for the June horse trials. Then we sped over the River Nene, and by the Museum of Leathercraft: tanneries by the waterside made Northampton a shoe-making centre (here 15,000 pairs of shoes were made for Cromwell's army, which is why later Charles II had its castle destroyed; and shoes for celebrities from Victoria to Nijinsky came from Northampton). The façade of a very fine 17th-century church proclaimed that Charles II gave 1,000 tons of timber for its rebuilding – his earlier wrath forgotten. There was a fleeting view of the market place and of old houses beleagured among graceless modern blocks, and then we paused in the cavernous gloom of the city's modern coach station (why it had to be made so depressingly short of daylight is a mystery).

Here the scheduled ¼-hour stop lengthened into nearly an hour while passengers fidgeted impatiently. Engine trouble, we were told. (This was the only instance of a mechanical hold-up which I encountered in the course of all my coach travels.) At last we were off again, and on a road that was more interesting than the M1, taking us through undulating and leafy ways, and by cottages and neatly laid drystone walls of an attractively warm-coloured sandstone. On the huge blue expanse of Pitsford Reservoir the tiny scarlet triangles of sailing dinghies made a colourful picture.

High up in Brixworth we passed the tall spire of a part-Saxon church – one of the finest in England – and a scatter of Georgian houses, then came a great farm, several country inns and a succession of majestic views to hills far beyond the fields of sheep or wheat, or of newly sown earth guarded by scarecrows.

Lamport Hall is a huge 17th-century mansion with realistic white swans flapping their wings on its gateposts. Beyond cottages with lattice windows, a signpost points to the battle site of Naseby where in 1645 the fate of Charles I was determined. Another stately home, Kelmarsh Hall, lay hidden behind great banks of vivid rhododendrons. The road wound its way on, rarely straight or level, past orchards and pretty cottage-gardens until we reached Market Harborough, and there stopped beside the river.

This is an attractive town, with a chequerboard square in the centre, a 17th-century hall (pillars below, pargetting above – decorative plasterwork), a fine church with a steeple that is exceptional even in a region of steeples, coaching inns and some handsome houses with wrought-iron verandahs overlooking the wide street. The house where Charles slept before the Battle of Naseby still stands. Wildflowers fringe the banks of the River Swift.

Once more out into the countryside where black lambs were basking in the sunshine, and there was a succession of sparkling rivers along the way, seen over the tops of low, neat hedges that had been properly trimmed and layered in the old craft way, and not hacked back by those chopping-and-tearing machines which ruin so many hedges now. The verges, too, had been left in their natural state and were brimming with wildflowers. At Great Glen, villagers sat on the benches of the triangular village green to enjoy the sun, the wallflowers and the mellow houses around.

As we approached Leicester the road widened, the traffic increased and the coach speeded up again. We were entering through the pleasanter suburbs of the city, where the smell of new-cut grass rose from the huge greens dotted with small boys in cricket whites; and, through fine wrought-iron gates, beds of white tulips looked equally well laundered. The museum with classical façade, and rows of demure little cottages with their date (1836), were almost the last touches of bygone Leicester before towering office blocks, multi-storey car parks and knitwear factories took over, dwarfing what is left of the old keep in the middle of Leicester, a group of almshouses and St Margaret's church. Much of this huge city centre is on an inhuman scale: colossal, featureless buildings reducing the population to ant-like proportions.

I dozed as the coach plodded on through the industrial outskirts, waking only at Loughborough. Here and further on there are occasional views of the canal system and its locks, colourful motor launches, and cows ruminating beneath willow trees; but for the most part this was a dull stretch of the journey, with nothing more interesting to look at than the great cooling towers steaming away in the middle distance.

And then came a respite from this tedium: an avenue of azaleas and rhododendrons, and the handsome buildings of Nottingham University. Soon we swung round the foot of the extraordinary sandstone outcrop (riddled with caves, like Gruyère cheese) at the heart of Nottingham, and thence into the middle of the noisy shopping centre where the coach station is sited (with the Tourist Information Centre near). I was late, tired, hot and cross: not at all predisposed to think well of the unknown city I was about to visit.

Saturday with Byron and Robin Hood

I had come to Nottingham for a particular purpose, which makes this chapter different from the others.

In this city – as in many others like it – the big hotels cater mainly for businessmen who sleep there only on weekdays, leaving the hotels empty from Friday to Sunday. Increasingly, therefore, such cities are trying to attract tourists at the weekends – not only by offering 4-star accommodation at a 2-star price but including all sorts of sightseeing opportunities in the offer. And obviously it makes sense to set off for such a weekend by coach not car if, throughout one's stay, one is transported about by coach – with that, too, included in the price. At the end of this book I list a number of these city weekend breaks; but only where Nottingham is concerned can I vouch for the excellence of what was provided and its value (for this year's 'Away Break' rates, tel. 0602 40661).

There were about 30 people who had booked, including two children. Like me, many thought of Nottingham as simply an industrial city and were not too sure whether a stay there was going to be entirely a pleasure. It turned out to be a memorable weekend: a really first-rate programme, a generous pack of booklets, good food and service for a reasonable price. And, a happy bonus for me, the Stakis Victoria Hotel, where we were based, is close by the coach station.

On Friday evening, a drink and an illustrated talk brought everyone together before changing for a mediaeval banquet (anyone so inclined was lent appropriate costume) consisting of game soup, help-yourself spare-ribs in barbecue sauce, a whole poussin, syllabub and cheeses, with mead and mulled wine. Meantime, Friar Tuck, assorted jesters and knights entertained the company. Even I, who had arrived late and cross, began to cheer up.

Next morning a coach with two lively young couriers took us to the castle perched 150 feet above the city (floodlit at night), past two of the most ancient inns in Britain (the Salutation and the Trip to Jerusalem) and a much-photographed statue of Robin Hood. The so-called castle, surrounded by pretty gardens with a bandstand and viewpoints at every turn, is in fact an Italianate mansion of the late 17th century which was the home of the Duke of Newcastle, replacing the mediaeval royal castle that used to stand here. An excellent guide took us round, naming the distant buildings and showing us Mortimer's hole, down which the more intrepid tourists can clamber. This is the 100-yard tunnel through which supporters of the boy-king Edward III entered to seize his widowed mother and her lover Mortimer who had been responsible for the particularly horrible murder of his father Edward II. The porous and very soft sandstone on which the castle stands, with former marshes around, is riddled with holes like a sponge: some enlarged as stores, one as a rifle range; the 'blood hole' is where infectious patients used to be isolated; in another, erring monks were imprisoned. Many Nottingham houses have huge cellars gouged from this easily worked stone, all at an unvarying 68°F. There were people living in rock dwellings right up to 1968.

The house is now an arts museum. We spent an hour and a half exploring just a few of its treasures – from kitchen gear of 1320 (pipkins, pitchers and – for breadmaking – pancheons) to the largest hoard of mediaeval gold ever found. For its sheer beauty, the collection of glass held many of us; and there is an exceptional collection of antique jewelry too, including an unforgettable pair of earrings, each with a decorated jasper urn captive inside a crystal bubble. Strangest of all: a 17th-century tortoiseshell casket containing twenty mourning slides – tiny mementoes, with initials and skeletons or other symbols of death, to be worn on a ribbon around the neck. On through galleries of silver, pottery, militaria and paintings we wandered, to end up with cups of coffee in the museum's attractive buttery, which has far views through arched windows, before walking downhill to the cobbled lane of old houses where the costume museum stands, with the Lace Centre in a half-timbered house close by.

Lace-making has been important in Nottingham for centuries; and this centre is the place to go for an appropriate souvenir (anything from a wall-hanging of lace down to a collar, frilly garters or handkerchief – or else buy a bobbin kit to make your own). In the museum there are period room-settings to show off costumes – the Georgian squire with port and pipe, crinolined Victorian ladies among their whatnots and davenports. Galleries of fal-lals are packed with fans, undies, handbags and buttons: the fans with microscopic embroidery on muslin, or made of fretworked horn, or with paintings on feathers; cotton drawers of 1900 succeeded by the pink silk crêpe of the 1930s. How many pricked fingers went into the making of schoolchildren's test pieces (meticulous darning and button-holing); and whose eyesight was strained while stitching by candlelight the vast tapestry map that shows all the villages of Nottinghamshire in 1632?

Only a few yards away, the old Brewhouse, too, has a story to tell. As well as relics from its brewing days exhibited in cellars gouged from the sandstone, it recreates the daily life of a century or more ago, in a bedroom, two kitchens, and a chemist's shop with blue jars and green bottles, essences of frangipane and patchouli, pills (Zox's 'death to pain') and potions (Rooke's Solar Elixir). There is a leisure room with a strange cross-section of pastimes (half-forgotten children's games like diabolo and bandalore, a box of cockfighting spurs). One room is devoted to a history of shaving, another is full of Valentines. Mementoes of the Second World War are in yet another of those famous sandstone cellars below the house.

But I think everyone's favourite among this cluster of museums was the old School House, a few yards away. It recreates one of the first 'ragged schools' (set up before compulsory education, when the first task of any school was to provide adequate clothing), and is now filled with trifles salvaged from the past. As we lifted up each desk-lid in turn – ink-stained, and carved with the names of long-departed Terries and Henries and Hughs – we found inside every one a different display. There were examples of copper-plate handwriting, smudged exercise-books devoted to labours with vulgar fractions, and well-thumbed atlases with half the world coloured an imperial red.

It was time to embark in the coach again, to hurry along Mansfield Road (where many of Nottingham's smaller hotels are) and so out into the countryside for an excellent light lunch with aperitif and wine, at Newstead Abbey, reached at the end of a long winding drive flanked by brilliantly colourful rhododendrons.

The Abbey ruins, and the house built onto them, are surrounded by a vast park with lake and waterfall (at each end of the lake is a mock-fort, built by the fifth lord who conducted miniature naval battles on the water), a rose garden and a Japanese garden. Little remains of the abbey, destroyed on the orders of Henry VIII, except for the very wide and beautiful west front. The estate was bought by the Byron family who built their house around the former cloister, resulting in an unusual mixture of monastic and domestic architecture. The poet Byron loved the family home but, with debts mounting, was forced to sell it in 1817.

We entered through the former crypt where painted alabaster monuments are housed under the rib vaulting (Nottingham was once a centre for alabaster carving). In the former cloisters is a herb garden with fountain, and the mediaeval chapter house still stands, too – now a chapel, colourfully decorated with stencilled flowers and emblems. There is a small who-did-what exhibition of monastic life, detailing the roles of cellarer, infirmarer, precentor (librarian), sacrist (maintenance), kitchener, succentor (ceremonial); and the daily routine, from midnight mass right through to 9 p.m. each day.

We moved on, in time as well as space, to the heyday of the Byrons – with the poet's lordly fourposter (swagged and tasselled, gold and black) and elegant wallpapers transforming what had been rugged stone walls in monastic days. The most interesting room is the Byron gallery with some of the poet's clothes, exotic costumes, sports gear (although lame, he was skilled in fencing, shooting, swimming and boxing), memorabilia of the many women in his life, his manuscripts and his racy letters (even his handwriting is impetuous). Of Newstead Abbey itself, in the years when he could no longer afford its upkeep, he wrote:

> Through the cracks in these battlements loud the winds whistle,
> For the hall of my fathers is gone to decay;
> And in yon once gay garden the hemlock and thistle
> Have choak'd up the rose, which late bloom'd in the way . . .

There was still more to see, such as the crimson salon with aquamarine ceiling and panels of birds and flowers, where concerts are held (Byron's own Hebrew Melodies are sometimes played on a piano of his time, or Christmas carols sung, for instance); and the great baronial hall with banners and minstrel's gallery. But we had to press on.

The route to Sherwood Forest was an attractive one: bluebells and broom blossomed in the wild, lilac and peonies in gardens. There were occasional glimpses of collieries' winding-gear beyond the trees. Walkers in orange anoraks pored over damp maps during a brief shower. Bowlers and cricket players were out in their white clothes undeterred by the rain; and a bride in white posed at the church door to be photographed with her groom. On the fringe of Sherwood Forest a fair was in full swing. Typical Saturday scenes.

We parked close to the Forest's interpretation centre and café (from which nature trails and guided walks set out) before scattering separately among the great oaks and yews of the forest. Most visitors headed for the 1,000-year-old Major Oak (within the hollow 36-foot trunk of which Robin Hood reputedly hid), after going through the labyrinth of the Robin Hood exhibition which tells in displays and ballads all the old legends of this favourite among folk heroes. Maid Marian is there of course ('a smurkynge wench . . . none of these coy dames') but so also is more substantial evidence about real life in the 1320s: the miller's work, village relationships, inside the castle, the use of the longbow. There is an audiovisual show, too, to explain the life of the 400-acre forest today: part of it is a Site of Special Scientific Interest with unusual insects, deer, and sixty species of birds (best spotted in April when the trees are not too leafy). Alas, since this visit, vandals set the Major Oak on fire, jeopardising its survival. There was an hour-and-a-half for wandering before returning to the coach.

We went back to Nottingham via beautiful Clumber Park (National Trust) where drifts of bluebells could be seen in the woods beyond the avenues of limes, to return to the hotel for dinner. Most of us felt it had been a full day; but some still had enough energy left to see Danny La Rue at the theatre, others to explore a few of the innumerable pubs which are a feature of Nottingham, noted for the number of its breweries.

Sunday with D. H. Lawrence

Next morning, we were joined by two honorary officers of the D. H. Lawrence Society, to point out as we travelled the villages, farms and churches which appear (under other names) in Lawrence's books. 'Nottingham, that dismal town . . .', he had written – but he loved the country around it. We saw, in the city, the college where he got his teaching diploma (an unprecedented achievement for a miner's son); went past the park where the annual Goose Fair is held, described in his story about the fair, and paused in the village of Cossall, described in his book *The Rainbow*. Here stands the home of Louise Burrows who was his fiancée for two years: the Burrows (whom he renamed Brangwyns), the church and the nearby marsh are all in the book. In the church we saw carvings made by Louise's father, listened to the organist playing (the church is affiliated to the Royal School of Church Music), and then strolled among the old cottages and lozenge-paned almshouses so well preserved that the village recently won a European conservation award. It would have been easy to spend several hours here, exploring footpaths and canalside.

A little way on we had views of the spot where Lawrence parted for ever from Jessie Chambers (Miriam in *Sons and Lovers*), Greasley Church and the surrounding hayfields (described in *Love among the Haystacks*), Moorgreen Reservoir (the drowning in *Women in Love* was based on an actual incident here) and the farm where he stayed to recuperate when 19 and found so much happiness with the Chambers family. 'That is the country of my heart', he wrote. 'The little red farm, where I got my first incentive to write. Jessie launched me like a princess launching a ship.'

We paused, too, outside Moorgreen Colliery (the 'mine among the cornfields' in *Sons and Lovers*), before visiting the miner's cottage, one of a terrace, where Lawrence lived from the age of 2 to 6. It has been furnished with items from the 1880s given by local people, many of whom remembered the Lawrence household. Gas lights burn, there is a rag rug on the tiled floor in front of the range and a tin bath hangs on the wall. The privy is still at the end of the garden. (The upper floor is a self-catering flat, available to rent for holidays: 051 653 8710.)

Lawrence's mother insisted on a move to a better house and we looked at this too, with its valley view of 'one vast cockleshell' of green, where he lived until 18; at the Three Tuns (which he renamed the Moon & Stars in *Sons and Lovers* and which now has a D. H. Lawrence bar lined with memorabilia); at Greasley Board School which he attended; at his aunt's cottage (this he put into *The Widowing of Mrs Holroyd* – by now, we were all wishing we had brushed up our reading before we came!); and finally – after a light lunch – we stopped at his birthplace in Eastwood.

Here his mother had a small shop in the front parlour for Nottingham lace and babywear which she made. The window has again been filled with such things, including a tucked bonnet bought from her. There's an inkwell Lawrence made from a lump of coal, miner's kneepads and 'snap-tin' (for bread-and-dripping or bread-and-jam) and a photograph of Mrs Lawrence in her thirties looking as careworn as if she were 60. The house is a small Lawrence museum; and around the corner is a cluster of craft workshops of which Lawrence would surely have approved. We left Lawrence country for the last visit of the weekend: Wollaton Hall. This tremendous Elizabethan mansion now houses a museum – or, rather, two. In the outhouses is an industrial museum (the first lace-making machine, attacked by Luddites in 1808; and early telephones and typewriters – among much else); while in the stately rooms themselves is a huge natural history museum of considerable distinction. There are some bizarre combinations – a stuffed giraffe soaring above one's head is dwarfed by the height of the hammer-beam roof, embellished with grotesque heads, in the great hall where it stands. The stuffed badgers in their setts seem extraordinarily real – while the bees and ants *are* real, viewed through Perspex domes or panels, as busy as Nottingham streets at the rush hour. The 800-acre grounds alone deserve a day's visit: gardens with statues and fountains, deer park, a lakeside nature trail, camellia house and varied events from flower shows to veteran car parades or international archery contests.

It had been a weekend packed with incident and variety. Exhausted but well pleased, we piled back into the coach to return to the Victoria Hotel for a substantial tea, with just enough time left for me to catch my homeward-bound coach. Of all the towns I had so far visited for this book, Nottingham had been the greatest surprise: the one at which I had expected least and found so much!

SOME MORE PLACES TO VISIT It is possible to stay on at the hotel for a third night at half-price, giving the opportunity to visit more of the area, on one's own; or, of course, to visit Nottingham independently of the Away Break scheme. For bus timetables with route map, tel. 0332 372078. For route map of city buses, tel. 0602 55745.

Blidworth and Papplewick (bus no. 141). Grave of Will Scarlet and Maid Marian's home at Blidworth. Forest wardens' graves and water-pumping station at Papplewick. The latter, plus smithy and miniature railway, opens on summer weekends and sometimes works. Café.

+Colwick Country Park (buses no. 80, 81). 300 acres by River Trent. Water sports on two lakes. Large marina.

Eastwood (buses no. 231, 332, 333). See text.

Georgian Nottingham (many bus services go to Weekday Cross). Use the Georgian Trail leaflet (see TIC below) to explore this area of Nottingham.

+Holme Pierrepont (bus no. 85). Hall. National Water Sports Centre. Country park.

Hucknall (buses no. 341–5). Market town. Byron's grave.

Lace Market (many bus services go to Weekday Cross). Use the Lace Market Trail leaflet (see TIC below) to explore the most ancient quarter of Nottingham.

Lenton (many bus services). Use the Lenton Trail leaflet (see TIC below) for a 1-mile walk through this conservation area where a village grew up around a priory.

Longdale (bus no. 63 to Kighill and 10-minute walk). Rural craft centre and working crafts museum. Café.

+Newstead Abbey (buses no. 62, 63). See text.

+Nottingham Arboretum (buses no. 108, 109). Lovely flower gardens (especially dahlias), aviary, fountain, etc. Café in summer.

Nottingham & Beeston Canal (many bus services go to Trent Bridge). A trail follows the most interesting 1¼ miles to Castle Lock where there is a Canal Museum – and excellent fish-and-chips! Return by bus or walk; or walk on to Lenton or Beeston, and return on buses no. 11, 12, 13 and 14. There is a canal guidebook (see TIC below).

+Nottingham Castle and museums (many bus services). See text.

Ruddington (bus no. 101). Hosiery Museum, with dwellings as well as workplaces of the Victorian knitters (open Wednesday evenings). Also Edwardian shops and school.

+Rufford Abbey, Edwinstowe (buses no. 33, 36). Craft centre, abbey remains and country park with lake. Café.

Southwell (buses no. 311 or 312). Famous minster. Market town.

+Trent Bridge (several bus services). For boat trips, boat hire and riverside promenade. Gardens, paddling pool, café.

+University Park (buses no. 12, 13, 14).

Huge boating lake, sports fields, paddling pool, rhododendrons and azaleas, café.

+Wollaton Hall (buses no. 21, 23, 321, 322). See text.

All the above can be visited nearly every day of the year except for Newstead Abbey (closed in winter).

SOME ANNUAL EVENTS May County agricultural show. **June** Festival (arts, sports, etc.). **July** Rose show. **Aug.** Mediaeval market. **Sept.** City Show. **Oct.** Goose Fair: about 800 stands. **Nov.** Music and drama festival.

TOURIST INFORMATION CENTRE 18 Milton Street (0602 40661)

Publications obtainable from the Centre include: Nottingham: Where to Go and What to See (10p); Nottingham (10p); Story of Lace (10p); Goose Fair (free); Nottingham's Pubs (50p); Museums in Nottingham (free); Trails – Georgian, Lace Market and Lenton (10p each); Nottingham and Beeston Canal (30p); brochures about Castle, Wollaton Hall, Newstead Abbey, Sherwood Forest, Robin Hood (10p each); D. H. Lawrence and D. H. Lawrence birthplace (free); The Country of My Heart – local guide to D. H. Lawrence (80p); What's On, monthly, and museum events (free); leaflets on shopping, nightlife, accommodation, city history, geology, eating places, the Council house, caves (all 5p). Disabled Handbook (20p).

The Centre has details of city guides; guided tours of caves, Castle, Wollaton Hall, etc; coach excursions; boat trips.

ECONOMY TIPS Accommodation Apart from the Away Breaks described in the text, there are other package or weekend rates. **Transport** Two city-centre bus services are free. They go near castle, museums, canal, Lace Market and Georgian areas. Easy Rider is a 2- or 4-week travel pass. Explorer tickets (see p. 206) cover journeys as far afield as Chesterfield (museums, etc.), Sheffield (see p. 167), Worksop (priory and museum), Southwell (ancient minster). Several are very scenic routes. **Admissions** Of the sights I have described the following are free: Brewhouse Museum, Costume Museum, Castle and Wollaton Hall (small charge on Sundays), Canal Museum and the country parks.

EARLY-CLOSING DAY Thursday (but some shops close on Monday).

MARKET DAYS There are five general markets, open on some or all weekdays. Cattle markets on Mondays and Saturdays.

LOCAL ALE Shipstone, Home, Kimberley.

TO PENZANCE
From Plymouth

Coaches depart about twice a day and the journey takes just under 3 hours. It goes through typically Cornish scenery of high moors alternating with woodlands and fields. There are glimpses of china-clay and tin mining, rivers, valleys and viaducts; and flowers by the roadside. A good stop on the way would be Truro, a Georgian town with a celebrated museum and a great cathedral: the river boat-trips are particularly enjoyable.

The coach, once it had shed the outskirts of Plymouth, crossed the Devon–Cornwall boundary at one of the best viewpoints in the west country – the long bridge over the River Tamar. This is side by side with Brunel's monumental achievement, the iron railway bridge on which he proudly had his name inscribed in huge letters (even though it is named after Prince Albert), together with the date when it was completed – 1859.

To allow naval ships to pass freely, the bridge had to be 100 feet above the river and cross it with a 300-foot span – but for reasons of economy, it is only wide enough to carry one rail-track. Travellers by train do not, of course, have a view of the bridge but one gets a splendid sight of it from the coach, and of its two 1,000-ton, curved trusses from which the track is suspended. When the first truss was floated out to be raised into position, a vast crowd watched this feat in a dramatic hush (Brunel insisted on silence) until, the tricky manoeuvre completed, a Royal Marines band burst into 'See the Conquering Hero Comes', accompanied by a storm of cheers. Later, a popular song celebrated the opening of the bridge with a chorus:

> From all parts of England you'll now have a chance
> To travel by steam right down to Penzance.

But Brunel the tireless did not live to make that journey across the bridge himself: worn out, he died that year aged only 53.

From high up on the modern road bridge, the sailing-boats and barges on the wide blue waters of the Tamar far below looked like toys. Then on once more through undistinguished suburbs until the countryside was reached, with glimpses of stony-bedded streams, occasional watermills and mediaeval stone bridges. Often on the horizon there appeared distant church towers standing four-square and pinnacled, distinctive landmarks typical of this part of Cornwall. These mediaeval granite towers have a fortress-like strength about them, but are lightened by the delicate touch of the little crocketed spires that adorn the top. Signposts point to villages (hidden in the folds of the hills) that have splendidly idiosyncratic names such as Doddycross and Merrymeet, Widegates and Catchfrench.

The coach ran fast and smooth along a stretch of dual carriageway with fine views, to pause in the pleasant town of Liskeard where even modest terraced houses have pillared doorways, and the central square is surrounded by early Victorian houses stuccoed or slate-hung, with handsome detailing of doorways and broad eaves. Its fine church is the second largest in Cornwall. 'Lis' is Cornish for capital, and the place was once the capital of a Cornish king.

Onward once more, and as the road curved this way and that it brought into view white farms sheltering between hills and a huge railway viaduct of eight colossal stone arches spanning a deep valley. When Brunel built the railway to Penzance, he had to construct more than three dozen such viaducts – in timber, replaced in stone only when the line was doubled in 1908 – which were so dizzying that many people refused to travel across them.

As we went further west, the winding route grew steadily more attractive, with wild daffodils and primroses by the thousand growing on the banks by the road. The trees were in bud, cottagers busy in their gardens, lambs cavorting in the fields. The stone hereabouts is reddish, like the soil, and the drystone walls built from it and then topped with green turf soon attract colonies of equally colourful wildflowers. Woodlands alternated with uninterrupted vistas ending in a blue haze of hills far away. I was travelling in April: tulips and tulip trees were in bloom, camellias and flowering cherries too – about a month earlier than in more northerly parts of England.

Beyond St Austell, we continued alternately to zoom down into valleys and strive up hills. Now the views were of moors and of a strange, white, lunar landscape beyond, created by the immense tips (or 'burrows') from the mining of china-clay, one of Cornwall's major industries. The tips rear up in strange shapes, some like the pyramids of Egypt, one like Cape Town's Table Mountain. The fine white clay is simply granite that water has decomposed. It was discovered in Cornwall in 1746 by William Cookworthy and now a million tons a year are exported: no country except China itself has such fine china-clay. But for every ton produced, five tons of waste are added to the mountainous burrows.

Then, throughout the rest of the journey, there began to appear another of Cornwall's unique landscape features: the tall, abandoned chimneys of engine-houses, often ivy-covered and ruined, of the abandoned mines. From Roman times or before,

Cornwall was mined for its tin and other minerals, fortunes being made or lost as new seams were opened or old ones ran out.

The road wound its way on through lush green fields and hedges with tall trees. The coach's passing blew off the gossamer seedheads of dandelion-clocks. Occasionally there was (another very Cornish touch) a stone cross by the roadside, continuing a tradition that goes back to Celtic times. Through Trevellick (a picturesque street of cottages and small Georgian houses) we went past a wide river bordered by reed-beds and then along a serpentine road which wound as much as the twinkling stream with which it kept company. The hilltop views were superb, once we had edged our way past a minibus of 'Cornish Tartan Majorettes' from America which, laden with all their gear, was making heavy work of the hills.

Soon the coach rumbled over the granite setts of Truro, to draw up by Lemon Quay (from which there is a good view, beyond the roofs, of the cathedral's three spires – built a century ago). The county town of Cornwall, Truro is thronged with people on market day (Wednesday). An inn and a street are named after the 18th-century admiral Boscawen, known as 'Old Dreadnought', whose family seat was nearby.

The onward road continued over moors, still with those white china-clay tips in sight. 'Wheal Jane' and 'Wheal Busy' and 'Wheal Tehidy', said the signposts – wheal means mine. The ruined tin-mine chimneys were all about us now.

At last, a glimpse of blue sea to the right – it came and went in a tantalising flash. We were entering an industrial part of Cornwall, with few fields or woods from here on.

Redruth is the 'capital' of the tin-mining area of Cornwall. One of its most striking buildings is the huge Wesleyan chapel built in 1826: Cornwall has been strongly Methodist ever since Wesley rode on horseback, over the rough moorland tracks of the 18th century, to make repeated missionary tours throughout the country, preaching in the open air and attracting a tremendous following.

Up on the high barren tor of Carn Brea (the Cornish words

mean rocky hill), where granite boulders jut through the sparse heath, stand a castle and a monument which Sir John Betjeman has likened to a bedroom candlestick and candle. They kept appearing and disappearing from view as the coach wound its way on. The castle is a sham 'Gothick' folly, and the pillar is dedicated to a local benefactor, who died in 1835 and was buried in St Paul's.

On the way to Camborne we passed other monuments to mining past and present – a particularly fine engine-house with flywheel (preserved by the National Trust), more of those ever-present chimneys, the spoil-heaps and pit-head gear of one of the few active tin mines left, and the important School of Mines at South Crofty. Camborne itself, with its terraces of granite cottages for the miners (and yet another Wesleyan chapel of some grandeur), was the birthplace of Trevithick whose statue stands there, and after whom a local pub is named. He was the youthful inventor of the first railway engine which, in 1804, pre-dated Stephenson's by ten years though Stephenson got all the fame. Perhaps more significantly, Trevithick developed the beam-engines for which Cornwall became famous. By pumping water out of the many mines that would otherwise have remained unworkable, these engines completely transformed the scale of tin-mining in Cornwall at the beginning of the 19th century.

And so the last lap of the journey was reached. From the lofty windows of the coach, I could see over even south Cornwall's high hedges – green banks topped with bushes of golden gorse. Approaching Hayle and its estuary (hayle is Cornish for estuary) there are colossal towans in the distance – sand dunes higher than houses – and then (within an unlovely suburban sprawl) the coach ran alongside the river itself, where small boats were moored by stone jetties. Because the road twists itself round, the coach went twice under the same stone railway bridge here. The tide was out, so waders and gulls were busy feeding off the mudflats. Two swans sailed out on the steely-blue water in the distance.

After that it was a quick ride into Penzance, past houses alternating with fields (a fairground had taken over here, and 'Cockerell's Thrilling Musical Rides for All' was going merrily round). The road passes the heliport where nearby cows grazed unconcerned by the noisy comings and goings, and skirts the wide bay with the castle on St Michael's Mount dramatically dominating the scene; and so to Penzance, stopping right by the harbour.

The Waterfront and its Boats

The harbour still has its fishing-boats, though sometimes they are outnumbered by small yachts; and it sees the comings and goings of the sleek white ferry taking visitors across to the Scilly Isles, or moored by the lighthouse pier which, with another great granite jetty, shelters the harbour waters from what can at times be a very wild sea beyond. Once there was so much trade that a dozen countries kept consuls in Penzance. Once, tens of thousands of migrants departed from this harbour to start a new life in Australia or America. Now its liveliest scenes are early in the year when loads of narcissi and daffodils from the Scillies are unloaded here.

I walked along the quay, looking down into the dry dock where ships come for repair and at the huge red buoys brought in to the Trinity House depot for their regular overhaul. Out on Battery Rocks a sea-water bathing-pool has taken over the site where once guns pointed out to sea, and is overlooked by terraced gardens on the hillside. Penzance rises up steeply, and the only level walk is along the seafront. The early Victorian promenade extends westward nearly all the way to the next town – the busy little fishing-port of Newlyn – from which one can easily take a bus back. The beach here is pebbly – for safe, sheltered sands, one has to go in the other direction, towards Marazion.

Facing the sea is the Barbican crafts centre which was previously old warehouses but has now been turned into a series of workshops where you can watch craftsmen at work and buy their wares – silver, pottery, leather and what-have-you. Below is an aquarium containing examples of all the local fish – flat turbots undulating their way into the sandy bed to lie there camouflaged; great eels in tunnels specially made for them in rocks (head protruding at one end, tail at the other); yellow seahorses; anemones very, very slowly going walkabout; and crawfish that seem all eyes and feelers. An excited family came in, bearing a more exotic find – a two-foot leathery turtle they had just discovered washed up from afar on the beach (mum had inadvertently sat on it), for which they hoped the aquarium would find a home.

The Charms of Chapel Street

At the far end of the quay is a narrow lane called Coinage Hall Street, recalling the heyday of Penzance when, in the 17th century, it had the right (like Camborne) to assay and coin tin from the Cornish mines. The lane continues steeply upwards into Chapel Street, lined with so many 17th- and 18th-century buildings of interest that there is a 6-page leaflet describing them (listed below). They include restaurants, bookshops, guesthouses and antique or crafts shops. Among them are a Georgian hotel (the Union) from the gallery of which the victory at the Battle of Trafalgar was first announced; the Nautical Museum, which not only has finds from historic wrecks but a full-size section (four decks) of an 18th-century man-o'-war; the 13th-century Turk's Head with log fires and a smuggler's tunnel leading from its cellar bar; the beamy 16th-century Admiral Benbow inn and restaurant, crammed with colourful figureheads and other marine salvage retrieved by its diver-owner (look up on the roof for the effigy of one of the smugglers who reputedly used the inn as a hideout); and the most curious of all, the Egyptian House – named for the bizarre decoration of the façade, which looks like a colourful stage-set for *Aïda*. It was built in 1835 to house a geological museum, fell into decay, and was restored only ten years ago: the National Trust has a shop below and there are holiday flats above. Just off Chapel Street is the 'pen sans' (holy headland) that gave Penzance its name, where the parish church now stands on the site of an ancient chapel to which Chapel Street originally led. The present granite church, built in 1832, is a charming example of Gothick architecture, and from its peaceful, leafy churchyard there are fine sea views to sit and enjoy.

Quiet Byways and Backstreets

Also within short (though sometimes steep) walking-distance of the coach station is a network of quiet roads with pretty houses, interspersed with small parks that were once the gardens of mansions. I found the 'Town Trail' (listed below) a great help in wending my way through the maze of Regency and early Victorian terraces in stucco or granite to discover the pretty villas of Regent Square, the Morrab Gardens and their graceful fountain, some fine Georgian houses, Penlee Park (which has tree ferns and other subtropical plants in its fifteen acres, and an excellent museum of local history and wildlife) and ultimately emerging onto busy Alverton Road where the Geological Museum stands: well worth a visit for it illuminates so much that is the essential Cornwall, its rocks and minerals. From here it is not far to get back to the harbour and coach station, via Market Jew Street ('jew' is Cornish for Tuesday) which is dominated by a statue of Sir Humphrey Davy, inventor of the miners' safety-lamp, standing on the site of the house where he began his experiments.

SOME MORE PLACES TO VISIT For bus times and route map, tel. 0736 2274. Inland lie the wild moors and crags; the coastline to the north is rugged while that to the south has sheltered, sunny coves.

+**Cape Cornwall** (buses no. 510, 512). Fine sea views, with reef below.

+**Carbis Bay** (bus no. 517). Popular sandy beach and cliff walks. A very good fish-and-chip restaurant.

+**Goldsithney** (buses no. 502, 503). Museum of Mechanical Music.

+**Gulval** (bus no. 516). Pretty inland village, within the 'golden acres' market-gardening area.

+**Hayle** (bus no. 518). Popular resort on estuary with sailing-boats; huge sand-dunes about one mile beyond, and beaches. Bird gardens.

+**Lamorna** (bus no. 504). Sandy cove at the end of a woodland valley with wild-flowers.

+**Lands End** (bus no. 501). Dramatic cliffs and rocks, with two lighthouses in view. Restaurant (and good Cornish pasties) in the hotel.

+**Lelant** (bus no. 517). Village on the Hayle estuary, see above. Golf course by the sea. Model village.

+**Madron** (buses no. 511, 512). Inland village, particularly worth visiting on Trafalgar Day, around 23 October, when a special service is held.

+**Marazion** (buses no. 502, 503). Sandy, safe beach. From here one can visit St Michael's Mount – on foot at low tide, otherwise by boat – and the castle on top of it, owned by the National Trust. Several good restaurants.

+**Morvah** (bus no. 512). Moorland village, close to the coastal footpath and spectacular cliff scenery. Chun Castle, one mile.

+**Mousehole** (buses no. 508, 509). Picturesque fishing village with historic inns and cottages; small beach. The sea-bird sanctuary is a short walk uphill. Seafood restaurants.

+**Newlyn** (buses no. 501, 504, 508, 509). Old fishing harbour (a good place to buy crabs), with notable art gallery and a meadery.

+**Pendeen** (buses no. 510, 512). Light-house (open most afternoons) is a short walk. Also on this route: Geevor tin mine and museum (open to public), and Old Count House where the miners collected their pay, now a restaurant.

+**Porthcurno** (bus no. 504). Popular beach of white sand, clifftop paths, clifftop open-air Minack Theatre with performances in summer.

+**St Buryan** (bus no. 504). Village of historic and prehistoric interest, with one of the few notable churches in Cornwall (15th century).

+**St Ives** (buses no. 516, 517). Quaint and over-popular. Once a fishing village and still an artists' colony; cottages and cobbled lanes crowd up its steep sides; any number of museums, crafts shops, restaurants, etc. Golden, sandy beaches; surfing.

+**Sennen Cove** (bus no. 501). Popular and extensive white sands, surfing, sea-angling, lifeboat station (often open to visitors).

In *England by Bus* I have described in detail bus-rides in this area – the Penwith peninsula – and many of the places listed above.

For details about boat trips to the Scilly Isles, tel. 0736 2009; to St Michael's Mount, 0736 4424. Helicopters to Scillies, 0736 3871.

All the above can be visited at any time of the year except for the Barbican, aquarium, Nautical and Geological Museums, the castle of St Michael's Mount, Geevor tin mine, Sennen lifeboat house.

SOME ANNUAL EVENTS May Band Festival (or in Sept.). **June** Corpus Christie Fair. Midsummer bonfires. **Aug.** Regatta and swimming events. Carnival.

TOURIST INFORMATION CENTRE Alverton Street, Penzance (0736 2207)

Publications obtainable from the Centre include: Penzance and District Guidebook, with accommodation details (free); Penzance and District Street Maps (10p); A Day in Chapel Street (free); Penzance Town Trail (20p); Walks in West Cornwall (50p); events list (free); Discover the Lands End Peninsula (free); Antiquities of Penwith (45p).

The Centre has the times of coach tours, guided walks and coastal boat trips.

ECONOMY TIPS Accommodation Saga holidays for pensioners, early and late in the season. Youth hostel: Castle Horneck. **Transport** Family day-tickets to Scillies by boat (Mondays and Fridays only). Explorer tickets (see p. 206) cover the whole of the Penwith peninsula (St Ives, Land's End, etc.) and also Helston, The Lizard, Falmouth and Truro. **Admissions** Of the sights I have described, the following are free: Barbican crafts centre, Geological Museum, St Michael's Mount (but not the castle), Newlyn Art Gallery, lifeboat station at Sennen Cove, some of the museums, etc. at St Ives, seabird sanctuary at Mousehole, Pendeen lighthouse.

EARLY-CLOSING DAY Wednesday.

LOCAL FOOD Seafood. Pasties.

TO PETERBOROUGH
From London

Coaches depart approximately every 2 hours and the journey takes 2 hours from north London or 2½ hours from Victoria. It goes through the fertile plains of eastern England, Cromwell's country, with rural views all the way.

This northward route is one of the few that is interesting even during the first hour spent getting out of London from Victoria. It does not go through industrial or down-at-heel suburbs as some do, but skirts Belgravia, Mayfair, St John's Wood and Hampstead.

The coach started its journey along Elizabeth Street – still flanked by elegant terraces with wrought-iron balconies and window-boxes of trailing plants. This is a street of little hotels (handy for non-Londoners who are using Victoria coach station); among them are small shops of quality and bistro-style restaurants. Then the coach joined the traffic inching its way past the Rifle Brigade memorial and up Grosvenor Place which has the high garden wall of Buckingham Palace on one side and prestigious buildings of Portland stone and polished granite on the other – embassies, the headquarters of British Steel and suchlike. It skirted the green island of Wellington Place with its memorials to the Duke of Wellington and other heroes of battle; in the middle is the Wellington Arch of 1823 (the figure on top, of Peace in a chariot, was added just before the First World War). It sped past the Ionic colonnade (1828) of Hyde Park Gate, with copies from the Parthenon frieze in the middle, and past Apsley House, designed by the brothers Adam and once the Duke of Wellington's home (now a museum to him). Travelling up through one side of Hyde Park, there are views of the Achilles memorial to the Duke (cast from captured French cannon) and other sculptures on the lawns to one side, and of Park Lane's elegant buildings beyond trees to the right – delicate bow-fronted

Georgian houses (Disraeli lived in one) dwarfed by the most expensive of towering modern hotels. Around the Roman-style Marble Arch (intended, in 1828, to be the gate of Buckingham Palace until it was found to be too narrow for state coaches) shrubs were coming into bloom and ducks paddled among the fountains: a serene contrast with this spot's bloody past, for here was Tyburn – until 1783, site of executions and religious martyrdoms. Cromwell's body was dug up and gibbetted here on the orders of Charles II.

In Portman Square I caught a quick glimpse of the Wedgwood-blue plaques with classical figures on the corner house built by Adam in 1773 (now the Heinz Gallery of the Royal Institute of British Architects) before we made our way up Gloucester Place – as in Elizabeth Street, most of the attractive houses of 1810 (decorative fanlights above colourful doors, pretty balconies, lamp brackets, blue plaques showing where Victorian authors lived) have become small hotels. We passed the site of the original Lord's Cricket Ground of 1787, now Dorset Square, before going along Park Road, which is lined by the backs of Nash's Regents Park

mansions and the mosque with golden dome and minaret recently built for London's Arab community, to the present Lord's (to which the Dorset Square turf was removed in 1814), invisible behind a high brick wall opposite the classical church of St John's Wood and its flowery park.

Finchley Road, which begins with attractive early Victorian villas in their gardens, changed character as we went north – blocks of luxury flats being succeeded by a good shopping area, and then suburban houses veiled by lilac or laburnum.

After picking up more passengers outside Golders Green tube station, we moved off at gradually increasing speed and soon shed the northern heights of London to start the steady ride up the A1. Signposts stated simply To the North. This, once known as the Great North Road, was originally a main stagecoach route, and along the way there are still some old posting inns to be seen – one is now named after the road's most notorious highwayman, Dick Turpin.

Gardens and fine views back to London's rooftops (a surprise to see how many trees survive among them) were soon succeeded by fields and woodland, streams and glimpses of lanes leading to whitewashed villages and to cricket-greens. A traffic hold-up provided a few moments to enjoy the scene, white Queen Anne's lace in abundant flower beneath poplars lining the road.

The further we went, the more agreeable the views became: silver birches and rowans, nursery gardens, a splash of scarlet and blue on green (golfers making good use of the early sunshine), fields of new wheat or of seedlings, languid streams or rivers with colourful small craft, and many glasshouses. This side of England is heavily cultivated, for the dark brown soil is rich. The only problem is lack of rain, hence the many and varied water towers visible along the way.

The first thatched cottages of the journey came into sight – roof-ridges neatly scalloped, tidy 'eyebrows' sheltering the windows. After crossing the boundary of Cambridge, the fields became noticeably larger – almost prairie-like in scale. In some, hundreds of acres of rape were in brilliant yellow bloom.

There were fewer trees now, except where lines of them marked the route of a wandering stream. Signposts now began to refer to this fen or that. The rich black earth is part of the Great Fen, nearly 700,000 acres that was largely bog until it was gradually drained from Saxon times onwards, mostly in the 17th century. Draining meant that wildfowlers and watermen would lose their livelihood: Cromwell became their spokesman (before the Civil War) and thus acquired the nickname, Lord of the Fens.

Away to the right, dozens of tall red chimneys rose up like a petrified forest: brickworks. From the clay soil in the vicinity are made many of England's bricks; and later I was struck by the great variety of colours used in the new buildings of Peterborough that are built from bricks made here.

We approached the city via, first, a new industrial zone where every factory looks like a colourful plastic box of enormous size, featureless and neat. Then came a very interesting development, the brand-new community of Orton. A garden suburb has recently been created, using those bricks to good effect – soft browns and ochres well combined with dark weatherboarding – with brick-paved shopping precincts, wide greens, and plenty of roadside planting though the trees were still only saplings. Everything was on a human scale (no tower blocks) and Orton looked as if, when mature, it would be a very happy place in which to live.

And so to Peterborough itself, approaching it past a lake of swans, a river with boats and a lock, mansions among their cedars and lawns. Then suddenly, after a brief glimpse of the cathedral's towers, we arrived: drawing up to the surprise of a coach station that is right in the middle of Peterborough's newest achievement – a huge and spectacular shopping centre, all glass and marble, fountains and coffee-shops, gliding escalators and sparkling lights.

Through Quiet Streets

I had expected all the bustle of a thriving industrial city, but much traffic is now routed away; so, once I was clear of the Queensgate shopping centre and its vicinity, I soon found myself in peaceful streets. I headed for Priestgate and the city's museum, which I hoped would give me some idea of Peterborough's origins. The street is lined with the sort of handsome houses that soon get snapped up by solicitors and estate agents for their offices. Two are associated with Squire Cooke: he lived in one (now the museum) after leaving his estranged wife in the other, next door (its curious tower and spire were added after part of the house became a Congregational church in 1864).

Upstairs in the museum I found Victorian rooms and old shops recreated, and lingered over the tins and packets in the grocer's, bearing long-forgotten brand names and slogans: Mazza-wattee tea, Wills' Woodbines, Jiffy dyes, Servants' Friend black-lead, Bile Beans for Biliousness, Luton straw-hat stains, nightlights, and packets containing crystals and 'cat's whiskers' for wireless-sets.

The mysteries of archaeological digs and identification of strata are made clear in a careful reconstruction from a local site, inhabited by successive peoples for nearly a quarter of a million years; while another room is filled with exhibits from the local prisoner-of-war camp which, in 1797, held 7,000 French prisoners, some clad in distinctive yellow garments. Their rations are on a list here (not bad: 1 lb beef a day, 4 pints of beer, Gloucestershire cheese specified, and greens 'stripped of their outer leaves'). Some of the French got out of imprisonment by enlisting in the British forces; a number married Peterborough girls and their descendants bear French names to this day. Others earned money by making and selling crafts – not only the bone models I had seen in the museums of other towns which had a POW camp nearby but straw marquetry: delicate boxes and other trifles, their intricate patterns still gleam-ing. Only the cheapest of materials were available to the prisoners – hence such other crafts as paper flowers or carved wood. Of the Museum's many information sheets, I found the one about these prisoners the most interesting.

In 1856, the Crimean War and Florence Nightingale's efforts had made people conscious as never before of the need for proper hospitals, particularly to cope with (in Peterborough as in other cities) cholera and typhoid spread by sewage that contaminated the water supplies. The museum building became (until 1928) the town's hospital, and the rooms I was walking around had once been wards.

At the end of Priestgate is Bridge Street (with the Tourist Information Centre housed beyond the great portico of the Town Hall). This street was the original centre of the town, laid out by its Norman abbot in 1133. Turning right, I walked past restaurants and down to the bridge over the Nene. Here stands an old Custom House – from the cupola on top, a lantern guided ships in at night to unload on the riverside where now there are pretty gardens for picnicking while watching the pleasure-boats go by. The town's modern theatre stands on the embankment here, and theatregoers can stroll by the waterside during the intervals.

Cathedral of Two Tragic Queens

I retraced my way up Bridge Street, towards the cathedral's mediaeval gateway, the grooves of its former portcullis still visible. Across Cathedral Square stand the colourful buttermarket and guildhall, built during the 17th century to provide an upstairs meeting-place supported on columns, in the cool shade of which farmers' wives used to sell their butter and eggs, right up to 1926. Under the clock are the royal arms of Charles II. Among Cathedral Square's many other interesting buildings is a mock-mediaeval shop (Hepworths) with statues of men famous in the history of Peterborough.

Just beyond the square lies the spacious old church of St John's (built in the reign of Henry IV – his antelope emblem is over the south porch). The sound of its bells two centuries ago guided to safety a traveller called Wyldbore who was lost in a fenland fog: ever since, a special bell-ringing which he endowed peals out each March.

Turning from Cathedral Square, it is pleasant to walk through the gateway and into the quiet cathedral precincts surrounded by centuries-old buildings. For over 1,300 years, this has been a holy place – beginning with a Saxon monastery of such wealth that Vikings came upriver to pillage it. A Norman abbot took over after

1066, so repressive in his rule over the local population that the revolt led by Hereward the Wake followed – the last stand to be made against the Norman conquerors. The wooden town went up in fire, but was rebuilt to prosper once more.

The building of the cathedral started in 1118, with the Benedictine abbots' dominance over the area continuing until Henry VIII's dissolution of the monasteries in 1539. However, he let the cathedral survive, perhaps because Catherine of Aragon is buried there (though it did not remain unscathed, for Cromwell's troops desecrated and destroyed some of its finest monuments, its stained glass, and the tomb of Catherine, its position now marked by her Spanish and English banners overhead).

I stopped awhile to admire the great west front, added in 1237: each of its three immense gables houses the statue of a different saint – Peter, Paul and Andrew.

Inside all is space and clear light. One of the cathedral's great splendours is the painted wooden roof of 1220 (unique in England), immensely long and colourful. Press-button lighting and a mirror-trolley make it possible to study every detail of the saints and flowers that decorate it. Beyond lie the elaborately carved choir-stalls and a pale, luminous baldachino of Derbyshire alabaster over the altar: an illuminated focal-point when darkness falls.

There are mysteries associated with both the famous features of Peterborough Cathedral, the west front and the painted roof. Both depend upon certain optical illusions for their dramatic effect, illusions so subtle that it has taken a professor of optics to spot and explain them. It's worth buying, in the cathedral, 'The Leaning Front of Peterborough' and reading it carefully before looking around.

Another very special thing about the cathedral is its use of a local marble (quarried by a creek at Alwalton), distinctively marked with the fossils of oyster shells. The font is made from it, and also the sculpted tomb of Abbot Benedict.

Behind the altar, three centuries later, the building was extended with superb fan-vaulting probably created by the great craftsman of King's College chapel, Cambridge (and here concerts are held). Outside are quiet cloisters with lawn and well, in which to sit and reflect; above the porch is the treasury where historic silver is on display. And at the west end hangs this memorial above the tombstone of a gravedigger who died, aged 98, in 1594. (The two queens mentioned in it are Catherine of Aragon and Mary Queen of Scots, the latter brought here at night in a purple-and-black procession of candle-bearers, after her beheading at nearby Fotheringhay, but reinterred later in Westminster Abbey on the orders of her son James I.)

> You see old Scarlett's picture stand on hie
> But at your feet there doth his body lye.
> His gravestone doth his age and deathtime show,
> His office by these tokens may you know.
> Second to none for strength and sturdy limm
> A scarbabe mighty voice with visage grim
> Hee had interr'd two queenes within this place
> And this towne's householders in his live's space
> Twice over. But at length his own turne came.
> What hee for others did, for him the same
> Was done. No doubt his soul does live for aye
> In heaven though here his body clad in clay.

Light was fading. The sexton tolled the calling-bell for evensong, and the choirboys in scarlet-and-white filed into their places. Their young voices rose unaccompanied to fill the lofty chancel, followed by the surge of the organ which at its crescendo made the stones vibrate. Candlelight flickered on the mediaeval brass of the eagle lectern. At last, reluctantly, the last echo died away from those ancient pillared arches. Silence and darkness fell.

SOME MORE PLACES TO VISIT For bus times and route map, tel. 0733 54571. The most interesting scenery lies to the west, which is not so flat.
+**Alwalton** (many bus services). For East of England Show ground: see events list. Good food at the Wheatsheaf.

+**Castor** (buses no. 310, 311, X47). Magnificent church. Roman remains.
+**Crowland** (buses no. X07, 307). Abbey ruins and old bridge. Reputed burial place of Hereward the Wake.
Elton Hall (buses no. 265, 266, 267, 323, X65). 15th-century house. Tea garden.
+**Fotheringhay** (infrequent bus no. 311

to Nassington and 1 mile walk). Scant remains of castle where Mary Queen of Scots was executed.

Helpston (buses no. 379, 380, 381). Reached via Maxey (watermill and fine church). Cottage of John Clare, the peasant poet (privately occupied); memorial with his verses; grave. (His manuscripts, etc. are in Peterborough Museum which has an information sheet about him.) Inn food.

Holme Fen (bus no. 315). Nature trail.

Longthorpe Tower (buses no. 310, 311, X47, 399, 1). Mediaeval tower with painted interior.

+Nene Park (many bus services). 500 acres incorporating Ferry Meadows Country Park. Boat trips, walks, Roman remains, bird watching, a bluebell walk, miniature railway, Orton Mere (see below), golf, riding and water sports. Cafés and wildlife information centre.

+Nene Way From the city centre to Wansford Steam Centre there is a footpath by the winding river, going via Orton, Ferry Meadows, Waternewton, etc. The Nene Way Guide shows the points along it at which there are bus-stops, cafés, etc.

Northborough (bus no. 382). 14th-century manor and gatehouse, once the home of Cromwell's widow (who is buried in nearby church). Now a restaurant. Open-days once a month in summer, and guided tours with tea (tel. to book, 0733 252050).

+Orton Mere (many bus services). Lake, swans, canoe championships. Terminus of Nene Valley Railway. Crowded at summer weekends.

Oundle (buses no. 265, 266, 267, X65). Beautiful streets of limestone houses. Restaurants at Talbot Hotel and Tyrrells.

+Peakirk (bus no. 330). Reached via the pretty stone village of Glinton. Waterfowl reserve with over 100 species, attractively landscaped. Armchair viewing through picture-window. Brass-rubbing (pictures of endangered species) is available. Wall paintings in church.

Sacrewell Mill (buses no. 310, 311, X47). Working watermill and rural bygones. Open by appointment (tel. 0780 782222).

Stamford (buses no. 379, 380, 381). Perfectly preserved mediaeval stone town, full of interest, with innumerable inns, churches, old theatre, waterside walks, local museum and museum of brewing, etc. Market. Tudor mansion: Burghley House (bus no. 101); café, horse trials.

Thorney (buses no. 336, X36). Historic houses and church. Inn food at Rose & Crown.

Thorpe Hall (buses no. 310, 311, 384, 399, X47, 1). A Commonwealth mansion with formal gardens. For opening times tel. 0733 265820.

Thorpe Wood (buses no. 1, 2, 310, 311, 399, X47). Nature trail of ½ mile. Guide pamphlet available (free) from Tourist Information Centre.

+Wansford Steam Centre (buses no. 310, 311, 312, X47). Twenty working locomotives of the Nene Valley Railway on show here. Fields and river nearby. Rail trips back to Peterborough, or to Ferry Meadows (see above: Nene Park).

+Waternewton (bus no. 312, infrequent). Down Mill Lane is deserted watermill on the Nene. Site of Roman finds now in Peterborough Museum. Meals at Papermill restaurant and Haycock Inn, 1 mile away.

Most of the above can be visited nearly every day of the year but Wansford Steam Centre, Elton Hall and Burghley House close in winter.

SOME ANNUAL EVENTS March Wyldbore bell-ringing (St John's), see p. 106. Shire Horses Show. **May** Cathedral open-days (special tours). Children's pilgrimage. **July** East of England Show. **Aug.** Ponies of Britain Show. Expo Steam (vintage engines). Country Music Festival. **Sept.** Horse and pony events. Eurosteam (Wansford). **Oct.** Cathedral choral festival. Bridge Fair. **Nov.** Advent carols. Firework Fiesta. **Dec.** Christingle and carol services, procession of shepherds and kings, festival of nine lessons, etc. Fitzwillam Hunt (at Alwalton). 'Santa Specials' on Nene Valley Railway.

TOURIST INFORMATION CENTRE
Town Hall, BridgeStreet (0733 63141)
Publications obtainable from the Centre include: City guidebook which, among much else, has a map showing the whereabouts of the city's numerous sports and recreations, and details of nearby villages (30p); Welcome to Peterborough: good street plan, map of environs, lists of eating-places and accommodation (10p); Places to visit around Peterborough (5p); Places to Eat and Stay (free); What's On,

monthly (free); Town Trail (free); Ferry Meadows leaflet (free); Nene Way Guide (free).
The Centre has times of local coach tours, Nene Valley railways and summer cruises on the river (or tel. 0536 81803 for the latter).

ECONOMY TIPS Accommodation Saxon Inn hotel has bargain weekends that include golf, steam railway, etc. in the price (bus no. 399). **Transport** The Anywhere bus ticket covers a day's travel throughout Eastern Counties' area. For families, pensioners and children the Explorer ticket is better value, within its range (Spalding, Boston, King's Lynn, Sandringham, Hunstanton, Huntingdon, Cambridge, Ely, Wickstead Park – 140 acres of leisure pursuits). **Admissions** The museum and Ferry Meadows are free. There are discounts for pensioners at Peakirk.

MARKET DAYS Tuesdays, Wednesdays, Fridays, Saturdays; and Thursday evenings.

LOCAL ALE Greene King.

TO PLYMOUTH
From London

Something special in coach travel: a non-stop service with hostess, refreshments, w.c. and video films. Coaches depart approximately every 2 hours and the journey takes 4 hours. It goes through scenery that varies from plains to hills, by streams and rivers, and past meadows and orchards.

The normal (and more frequent) coach service to Plymouth takes 6 hours, stopping on the way. But in 1981, the 'Rapide' service was introduced by Trathens to supplement it; and this, at a slightly higher cost, clips 2 hours off the long journey. Since there are no pauses along the way, Rapide coaches have some seats replaced by a cubicle containing flush w.c. and wash-basin; and a uniformed hostess plies one with various hot and cold drinks, soup, sandwiches and other snacks. On two small screens overhead (one up front and one mid-way) a film is shown once the journey is under way: a rather old film, as a rule. On my trip, those who preferred silence were outvoted by those wanting the video turned on (some coaches have individual headphones); but as the windows were not curtained it was still possible to enjoy the view instead – which I preferred to watching a rather youthful Henry Fonda through the magenta thicket of two punk heads just in front of me. Certainly these diversions help to while away the boring bits of journeys which are inevitable when one starts out from central London and has all the suburbs to get through before the countryside starts. (Reading, letter-writing or a cassette-player with lightweight headphones are alternatives – if that lost art, contemplation, is not enough.)

The route to the west country is mostly along motorways: the M4 goes through Berkshire and Wiltshire to the Bristol Channel, and then the coach turns south along the M5 into Somerset to reach Devonshire's less busy roads.

Berkshire's landscape is sedate rather than spectacular. As we passed, rooks flew up from old trees burdened with ivy, pheasants pottered among the furrows of a newly ploughed field and, on a series of water-skiing lakes created from disused gravel-pits, coots swam busily about their affairs. This is an area where sandy soil (supporting pines, larches and silver birch) is succeeded by chalk, which yields up flints that go to make the characteristic walls of the county. Winter was only slowly giving way to spring: tender green shoots of wheat were thrusting up and daffodils grew wild on some banks, but still there was smoke drifting from many a cottage chimney.

In the distance rose the tower blocks of busy Swindon, slightly tinted by the sun's rays, but once they were out of sight the scene became wholly rural. We pressed on through green hills. More than once, we crossed the winding Avon, running clear and calm. Fields had dry-stone walls or hedges with hawthorn in full bloom, the

bright yellow flowers of coltsfoot at their feet. Then the sea came into view, and the high cranes of Avonmouth, Bristol's seaport.

Again, the local architecture changed with the changing geology: church towers, high and battlemented, showed the red sandstone at its most striking. The scenery became more dramatic as the route rose up above a vast plain, with great cuttings hewn from rock to give the road an easy passage through the hills. Down steep and wooded hillsides we went, into Somerset, county of rich brown earth and willow-lined streams. In this part of it, once marshy, great fields have been reclaimed for cows to graze on, but all are still criss-crossed with drainage ditches. Often streams ran beside the road, clogged by reeds or clumps of bulrushes (more accurately, reedmace), no longer brown and velvety but with their seedheads burst wide open and looking like ragged mops. The trees were still bare enough to reveal great round clusters of mistletoe high up, but in the fields there were already buttercups and daisies.

Around Tiverton we passed cider orchards, soon to become a spectacle of pink blossom; and then the flat landscape gave way to gently rounded hills through which the River Exe winds – wide enough for a small cargo ship to be making its way, as well as sailing-boats.

The coach swept across a heath with far-distant views and through the pines and birches of Exeter Forest. There were kingcups glowing at the brim of a pond, an old stone dovecote, cows patiently waiting to be milked and a mediaeval bridge before the rural tranquillity changed: a huge quarry of granite dominated one side of the road, clawed out of the hillside. But this was soon behind us, and there were still country scenes to enjoy – a donkey in an orchard, black-faced lambs, white farms with slate roofs, stone barns and stony beds to the many bubbling streams hereabouts, and in the background the wilderness of the moors – until at last the unappealing outskirts of Plymouth enveloped us.

Despite the speed of the coach (which regularly overtook others on the road) it had been a very smooth ride, the four hours hardly seeming so long. Rapide services have proved so popular that many are starting up elsewhere.

The Barbican which Drake Knew Well

Bretonside is the name of the street where the coaches stop, and this name explains in a word much of Plymouth's history. Facing Britanny and, beyond it, Spain, the town was vulnerable to attack from either of these countries. The Bretons so frequently set fire to houses behind the harbour that this area became known as 'the Breton side'. Right up to this century, Plymouth's history was therefore dominated by the need for sea defence against the French or the Spanish, which explains much of what one sees when walking around the older parts.

But it was from the air, and from a German enemy, that the most recent attacks came, devastating huge areas (which is why the heart of Plymouth consists only of modern buildings). Just north of the coach station the shell of a bombed 17th-century church has been retained as a memorial of that destruction.

To find what remains of historic Plymouth by the old harbour, I walked south – making a slight detour to visit the Merchant's House in St Andrew's Street first, because inside this fine half-timbered Tudor building is a well-mounted exhibition that explains how the town developed, from prehistoric times onwards. In the Middle Ages it was merely an outpost of Plympton (now just a suburb) where a great priory stood. Henry VIII improved Plymouth's fortifications and Charles II extended them still more. Now the action is farther afield – at the Devonport end of the town where there is a great naval dockyard, from which many of the task force ships sailed to the Falklands in 1982.

There's a replica of Drake's drum in the Merchant's House ('If the Dons sight Devon, I'll quit the port of heaven, An' drum them up the Channel as we drummed them long ago'): the real drum is at his home, Buckland Abbey (listed below). The Civil War siege of Plymouth by the Royalists is re-enacted in a diorama of model soldiers; and I particularly enjoyed mementoes of the merchant himself, mayor of Plymouth in 1601, who owed his wealth and honours to the capture of Spanish treasure-ships – until he was reported to be 'unfit for his work, being old and corpulent'.

Nearby Southside Street is the oldest lane in the Barbican

quarter ('barbican' means defence-works), lined with interesting shops and restaurants, historic inns, craftsmen's studios and old warehouses that were once stacked with casks of wine. The distinctive Plymouth gin is distilled here in ancient premises that incorporate a mediaeval hall once used by Huguenot refugees, and which can be visited. To each side are narrow cobbled opes – the local name for openings or alleyways between the high stone houses.

The granite quay around the Barbican overlooks a harbour busy with fishing-boats, and I bought plaice from the waterfront fish market which looks uncommonly like a Victorian railway station (not surprising since its designer was a railway engineer). Across the water is the big 'China House' where the first real china was made in England from fine white Cornish clay, lovely examples of which are displayed at the city museum. French prisoners of war were housed here during the Napoleonic Wars (some whiled away the years by making superb models – of ships, or of working guillotines! – from meat-bones, and these too are now in the museum). There's a story here of a ghost that cries 'Au secours'. A little further along is a jetty covered with plaques recording many historic embarkations from this point. But the most celebrated of all the migrants were, of course, the Pilgrim Fathers whose last sight of England in 1620 was from the *Mayflower* as she drew away from Plymouth. Over the *Mayflower* memorial fly the union flag and the stars-and-stripes, while a board on the house where the pilgrims stayed before embarking lists the names of those who sailed and their trades.

A narrow flight of steps opposite leads up to all that is left of Plymouth's earliest, mediaeval fortifications and thence to the famous Hoe (meaning 'headland').

Smooth Lawns Above the Sea

The Hoe, too, is only a short walk from the coach station (via Hoegate Street) or from the Barbican (up steep Lambhay Hill). After the jostle in the narrow lanes of the Barbican, I found it a relief to be up here where all is space and light – a tremendous expanse of feltlike lawns and flowerbeds with the great blue panorama of Plymouth Sound spread out before me, and sea breezes making the row of flags of all nations flutter gaily. This headland is deservedly world-famous. Often in the past it was the gathering place for citizens when an attack was expected, for archery-practice, or to watch executions. Now it is a promenade for holidaymakers picnicking on the lawns as they watch warships and sailing-boats in the Sound far below, or strolling to look at the many memorials (to Drake and other Devon sea heroes) and climb up inside Smeaton's red-and-white lighthouse of 1769, brought back here simply as a landmark when a new lighthouse replaced it on the lonely Eddy-stone rock 14 miles out at sea. Eddystone (meaning a rock round which the ocean currents eddy) is where the very first lighthouse out at sea was built in the 17th century. This one was destroyed, but Smeaton's – designed to the shape of an oak trunk, and made of interlocking granite blocks – was impregnable: storms split the rock but not the building. When a new lighthouse replaced it on another rock, it was brought here: a much-loved symbol of England, which used to be on our pennies until metrication changed them. Exhibits from both these early lighthouses are in the city museum.

At the Barbican end of the Hoe is the great, angular Citadel built by Charles II (and still garrisoned – you may see gun-training or other exercises going on) from the 60-foot ramparts of which I had even finer views of Eddystone, of Drake's Island, and of Rennie's mile-long granite breakwater completed in 1841, which is what turned stormy Plymouth Sound into a sheltered anchorage. It, and Drake's memorial, are floodlit in summer. (Other good sea viewpoints are the buffet-bar at the top of the Holiday Inn, and the top of the Mayflower Hotel. From the back of the Citadel, I enjoyed views over the city's rooftops to Dartmoor.) Below the Citadel is Plymouth's world-famous aquarium, belonging to the Marine Biological Assocation.

The other end of the Hoe stretches out in front of a terrace of stately stucco mansions, one of which belonged to Lord and Lady Astor when they were the city's lord mayor and MP respectively (this, and some of Nancy Astor's emeralds, were given to the city for use on ceremonial occasions). It is in this direction that some of the best hotels and guesthouses lie.

Drake's statue stands on the site of that famous game of bowls, and bowls are still played on the Hoe. It is also the place where all the world and his wife congregate to watch sea races and the air show; or the Lord Mayor's procession wending its way along the promenade each year.

Armada Way and Royal Parade

Standing in the centre of the Hoe and looking inland, I saw a tremendous vista cutting a green swathe right through the modern heart of Plymouth to the rail station nearly a mile away – lawns, flowerbeds and fountains all the way. This imaginative use of space right in the middle of the busy city was made possible only because Plymouth was so dreadfully flattened by the bombing of World War II. Off Armada Way lie the principal shops, the Tourist Information Centre, the Guildhall with its stained-glass windows, and the high-rise Civic Centre, the rooftop of which provides yet another of Plymouth's spectacular viewpoints (there are often exhibitions in the Centre). Royal Parade crosses Armada Way: at its west end is the brand-new theatre which puts on plays of West End standard; to the east (in the direction of the coach station once more) is St Andrew's church with the Prysten (priests') House behind it. The parish was originally under the control of the big priory at Plympton and it is generally believed that the prior used this house on his visits, dispensing justice in its galleried court and using the ancient oak throne still on view. The old lattice-windowed house is itself well worth a visit, and in one room there's an exhibition of herbs (which one can buy). In another, a team of volunteers is usually hard at work on a 240-foot tapestry telling the history of Plymouth – they've been at it for six years so far. And in a third is a great model of Plymouth in 1620, the layout of its fortifications quite different but the Barbican lanes much the same as now.

The mediaeval church had to be rebuilt after bombing, but some of its monuments survived. Catherine of Aragon worshipped here, so did the Pilgrim Fathers. Drake's wife was buried here, and the great east window is a memorial to Nancy Astor. I liked two modern touches: the hassocks, each embroidered with a different wildflower of Devon, and the sound of the carillon floating out over the city.

Annually the American ambassador or consul comes to this church, and to the 'Door of Unity' by which the Prysten House is entered, for a special service. It commemorates the honour paid by the English to an American naval commander killed in the 1813 war between the two nations, who is buried beside that door.

From Gobies to Golden Globes

Plymouth's city museum (a few minutes' walk from the coach station) is exceptionally good – and varied. I spent a long time in the wildlife gallery where a typical rock-pool has been created with live gobies, hermit-crabs and brittle-stars; and was absorbed by the display of colourful limestones, each from a different local quarry, which I had been seeing on the façades of banks and other buildings in Plymouth. Upstairs is a silver replica of the 1698 Eddystone lighthouse, and a cutaway model of Smeaton's version – complete down to every bucket and bunk-bed. The Eddystone men were given medals exempting them from being press-ganged; the only one to survive the centuries is on display. Drake's silver-and-gold 'cup' is there: a globe supported by sea gods, commemorating his voyage round the world. There's a fine collection of Plymouth china; and another of Lely and Van Dyck portraits – including one of Philip III's son as a ruffed and bejewelled toddler in the 17th-century version of a pushchair. Altogether the museum is well worth a lingering visit (there are cafés nearby).

SOME MORE PLACES TO VISIT For bus times and route map tel. 0752 664011. Inland lie the hills and valleys of Dartmoor; to the east the mild and lovely South Hams area of Devon.

+**Antony House, Torpoint** (buses no. 75 and 86 are taken across on ferry). National Trust. Georgian mansion in grounds.

+**Buckland Abbey, Yelverton** (buses no. 55A, 55C). National Trust. Drake's home; a mediaeval abbey. Museum. Garden. Café.

+**Cotehele** (boat and short walk). National Trust. Tudor house, garden, museum, watermill, slide show, barge.

Dart Valley Railway, Buckfastleigh (bus no. 129). Scenic ride on steam train.

+**Dartmoor Wildlife Park, Sparkwell** (bus no. 58, 59). Acres of animals in freedom. Café.

+**Drake's Island** (reached by boat). The old fort is used for adventure holidays for youngsters. There is a sandy beach here.

+**Mount Edgcumbe** (buses no. 26, 27 to Durnford Street, then ferry). Tudor mansion; and country park with nature trail. Café.

+Saltram House, Plympton (bus no. 22 and a 1-mile walk). National Trust mansion.

+Saltash (buses no. 70, 71, 72, 76). Craft centre at Tideford; D-Day memorial.

+Shire Horse Farm, Yealmpton (bus no. 93). Horse parades, cart rides.

Wembury Mill Café (bus no. 48 and ½-mile walk). National Trust. Mediaeval mill on sandy beach.

+Yelverton village (buses no. 55A, 55C and 83–85). On edge of Dartmoor, with paperweight centre. Pub and restaurant.

The following close in winter: Citadel, Civic Centre roof deck, Drake's Island, Smeaton's lighthouse, Yelverton's paperweight centre, Antony House, Cotehele, Dart Valley Railway, Mount Edgcumbe (house), Saltram House.

Bus-riding around scenic areas: In summer, Dartmoor (north of Plymouth) has a double decker called the Transmoor Link (leaflet available from TIC). In *England by Bus* I have described bussing around the pretty South Hams area east of Plymouth. Plymouth has no sandy beach but bus no. 53 goes to those at Jennycliff and Bovisand where the underwater diving centre occupies a Victorian fort; also Wembury (see above).

Boats go to the following in summer (for details, tel. numbers given): dockyard with warships; rivers Tamar and Yealm; coastal cruise to Looe (0752 822202 or 0752 822797); Cawsand, sandy beach (0752 822797).

SOME ANNUAL EVENTS May 'Door of Unity' Service – see p. 118. Lord Mayor's Show. **June** Horse Show. Music week. **July** Sea races. Saltram Fayre. Music and crafts festival. **Aug.** Navy Days (dockyard open). Air Show (biennial).

TOURIST INFORMATION CENTRE Civic Centre, Armada Way (0752 264849) (In summer, there are Tourist Information Centres at 12 The Barbican and Millbay Docks too.)

Publications obtainable from the Centre include: colourful guidebook with map, accommodation details, etc. (free); street guide (free); Historic Walk leaflet – Barbican Hoe, etc. (50p); What's On, monthly (free); Inn Tour of Barbican (free); boat cruise leaflets (free); The Dartmoor Visitor (free).

The Centre has details of guided walks (including those at the naval base, on Drake's Island, in the Citadel; and on

Dartmoor); bus tours (including evening pub tours and open-top city tours); coach excursions; and cycle hire.

ECONOMY TIPS Accommodation Youth Hostel: Belmont House, Belmont Place. **Transport** See above. **Admissions** Of the sights I have described, the following are free: Barbican (and the distillery), Hoe, Guildhall, City Museum, Yelverton's paperweight centre and Mount Edgcumbe country park. There is a bargain ticket that covers three sights (and a walks leaflet): the Merchant's House, an Elizabethan house in the Barbican and Smeaton's lighthouse.

EARLY-CLOSING DAY Wednesday.

MARKET DAYS Pannier Market daily. Cattle Market (Plympton), Mondays.

LOCAL FOOD & DRINK Seafood. Devonshire cream. Cider. Plymouth gin.

TO PORTSMOUTH
From London

Coaches depart approximately every 2 hours and the journey takes 2 hours. It goes through the high places of the North and South Downs, forests alternating with heaths and far views. A good stop on the way would be the Georgian town of Petersfield or the Queen Elizabeth Country Park described below.

The coach swung out of Victoria coach station and sped towards Chelsea, passing the Scots Guards barracks and crossing colourful Chelsea Bridge with its golden galleons. There were golden touches in Battersea Park too – daffodils and winter jasmine – where ducks swam busily on the lake. After that it would, I knew, be well over half-an-hour before we were free of London's suburbs so I settled down to read the Portsmouth books I had previously ordered by post (listed below) until we had passed Guildford and its great modern cathedral dominating the skyline.

From then on there was scenery to enjoy, particularly when the road climbed up into hills from which there were distant views. In a green field, a newborn calf was being nuzzled by its mother, its black coat still shining wet. Whitewashed cottages around a village green were succeeded by sandy heaths with pines and gorse. The road snaked up and up, until we were speeding along a hillside with (on one side of the road) treetops level with the coach and furry catkins brushing its sides. We wound around the Devil's Punch Bowl, looking down into its tree-filled depths patterned with sun and shade. This was one of the National Trust's earliest purchases, saving it from being bought as a building site. It owes its curious formation to a number of springs that washed away the sandy soil until the clay bottom was reached. A roadside stone commemorates the murder of a sailor returning to Portsmouth in Nelson's time.

On through Hindhead and Liphook – small towns of antique shops and restaurants, posh schools and mock-Tudor mansions, rhododendrons and holly thickets. The air of these heights is reputedly healthful, made fragrant by pines, which accounts for the number of nursing-homes along the way.

The road takes a downward turn into Hampshire and little Sheet where plump white ducks were dabbling in a sparkling stream. The coach paused awhile in Petersfield, outside Dragon House, its handsome Georgian porch and brass knocker typical of the town's architecture. Ahead lay great, sleeping humps – the South Downs. Once more we wound our way upward. The sandy heathlands of Surrey lay far behind and here all is chalk: a bright, white cutting cloven from the green hillside let the road through. In the grassy fields were black-stockinged lambs, and gulls picking over ploughed soil were a sign that the sea could not be far away.

Quickly past Queen Elizabeth Country Park and a windmill glimpsed on the horizon, and soon the outskirts of Portsmouth came into view together with the shining water of a great natural harbour, small boats at their moorings and birds probing the mudflats. Ten minutes of ugly suburban sprawl followed, a whiff of hops blew in

(Whitebread's brewery stands where once ale was brewed for Henry VIII's navy) and then the coach drew up right by the historic naval dockyard, HMS *Victory* and the waterfront busy with tugs and ferries.

Historic Ships in the Naval Dockyard

One of the good things about visiting Portsmouth out of season is that, unlike some places, it keeps its most celebrated places of interest open all the year. Another is that many are close together, which means a lot can be seen in limited time.

HMS *Victory* is what brings most visitors to Portsmouth but by the time this book is published she will have a rival right next to her. *Mary Rose*. This amazing ship, resurrected after more than four centuries on the sea bed, was installed in 1982 with all the world's eyes on her: hundreds of television cameras and nearly a thousand journalists reporting the event.

Why the excitement? *Mary Rose* was the pride of Henry VIII's fleet, manned by a crew of hundreds. But calamity struck. While the king was watching his fleet sail out to prevent a French attack on Portsmouth, he saw the *Mary Rose* heel over, perhaps in a gust of wind, and, as her gunports were open, sink within minutes. The story of how one man's persistence led to the rediscovery, in 1967, of where she lay and how hundreds of volunteer divers worked on her excavation for twelve years is in itself dramatic; the actual raising of the ship was simply the grand culmination of much that had gone before. *Mary Rose* has proved to be a time-capsule, the mud having preserved every small feature of Tudor life as it was on that fatal afternoon in 1545, even down to the fingerprint of the ship's doctor in a jar of ointment and many pocket sundials – the Tudor version of wristwatches. Some of these unique finds are now on show here or in Southsea Castle.

As to HMS *Victory*, she has a very different story to tell. Seeing all her gilded and immaculate splendour now, it is amazing to recall that, before the Battle of Trafalgar, she had just been an old hulk mouldering away in the Medway estuary. Nelson spotted her, liked her lines, and got her refitted as his flagship – but even he could scarcely have guessed at the immortal reputation that was to be hers. He did not see the victory that was won at Trafalgar; the place below-decks where he died after a gunshot wound early in the battle is now preserved like a shrine. It was not, however, the story of that famous occasion which left most impression on me but the privations of the unnamed hundreds who served on board, the punishments and spartan shipboard life they endured.

Facing HMS *Victory* is the Royal Navy Museum, with more mementoes of Nelson as well as other naval exhibits.

Old Portsmouth

The Naval Dockyard dates from Tudor times. But Portsmouth was the coast's greatest stronghold long before that. A short walk or a five-minute bus ride (no. 15 or 16) takes one much further back in time – to the tip of Portsmouth Point. I got off, however, at the start of the old High Street which leads down to the Point in order to enjoy walking along it and looking at its Georgian and earlier houses, old inns and Portsmouth Cathedral, parts of which are Norman.

The Point was where Portsmouth began. It is ringed with towers, batteries and bastions which one can walk in or on, some dating back to the time of Agincourt. There are quaint buildings along its main street and in its alleyways and courtyards; and behind it lies the Camber, the sheltered anchorage (now busy with commercial shipping) where once lay ships waiting to take Richard Coeur-de-Lion and his crusaders to the Holy Wars. And it was from near here that the very first settlers embarked for Australia: there is a striking modern memorial to them.

From a seat at the end of the Point I sat watching today's shipping going to and from in the Solent on less hazardous missions, a breeze merrily flicking up small waves and setting the ships' flags dancing: ship-watching is not the least of Portsmouth's diversions.

Southsea's Beaches

And so to another bus (no. 15; or in summer, an open-topper, no. 25 or 26) and another scene, for Portsmouth is a city of contrasts. East of the Point there used to be marshes but, once drained, the area became an ideal spot for a seaside resort on this most sunny of coasts where the bathing is safe, though the beach is pebbly. In the time of George IV, Thomas Owen saw the potential and began to build. It is to his acumen and good taste that Southsea owes its handsome streets of Regency and early Victorian houses, biggish hotels on the front and small ones behind. But what I most enjoyed about Southsea is its unique 'green belt' – lawns, commons and flower gardens running for miles along the shore, more than compensating for the lack of sands on which to sunbathe or picnic. Among the gardens are diversions for children – boat ponds, a model village and so forth, and there are two piers.

It was on this stretch of shore that Henry VIII built his watchdog, Southsea Castle. I made my way up to its ramparts and looked out, as he had done from this spot, to the waters where the *Mary Rose* sank and imagined the reactions of that choleric monarch: perhaps it was just as well for the commander that he went down with his ship!

The exhibitions inside the castle are excellent, making plain how Portsmouth and its fortifications developed over the centuries.

This is another good spot from which to watch all the big ships that throng the Solent on their way to Portsmouth or Southampton. Each day the nearby Tourist Information Centre puts up details of major vessels that are due to pass.

Eastney and the Royal Marines

Still further east is Royal Marines' territory (reached by buses no. 3, 4 and 15–18). The public are allowed into the barracks to see their award-winning museum, overlooking lawns and seafront: another good picnicking spot. The Victorian building is palatial, its decorative ceilings and staircase brilliantly coloured and gilded: the museum would be worth a visit for this alone. As to the exhibits, I'm not sure what I found most absorbing – some ancient ships' biscuits, iron-hard and indestructible enough to have survived since 1820; or the vivid audiovisual recreation of the battle of Zeebrugge in 1918, with tiny models and realistic sound-effects.

Close by the barracks is another monument of the Victorian era, the century-old pumping station. Its purpose was utilitarian – the shifting of Portsmouth's sewage out to sea – but the Victorians were rightly proud of their achievement in bringing sanitation to teeming cities previously honeycombed with typhoid-laden cesspits, and they built their pumping-stations with panache, like temples of engineering. When Mike Thomas was a schoolboy thirty years ago, he used to stand outside and watch through the windows the massive steel pistons gliding rhythmically up and down. But in 1954 they stopped: designed to pump 300,000 gallons an hour, the coal-fired steam engine could not cope when the expansion of modern Portsmouth resulted in millions of gallons, a task for diesel. The end of the story? Far from it, for the beam engine has recently been restored, the gleaming pistons pound away once more and now in charge of one of the city's most popular exhibits is Mike Thomas.

Hayling Island: Sands and Wild Places

Just beyond Eastney is a ferry to take passengers over to Hayling: it is at the bus terminus of the open-topped no. 25 or 26 which runs along the Southsea shore. Waiting on the other side of the water is another open-topper (no. 333 or 702) to take you from there to the further side of the island, unless you prefer to walk along the beach. Unlike Southsea, the Hayling coastline is sandy: this is the place for children's bucket-and-spade activities when the tide is out.

In between amusement parks are quiet stretches of heath and sand, but the parts of Hayling I most enjoyed were to the east where byways lead to Chichester Harbour and wild spots frequented only by birds, fishermen and small sailing-boats. The no. 300, 301 and 302 buses wander up country lanes on this side of the island and it is a simple matter to hop off at one point, picnic basket and binoculars in hand, to find one's way to the waterfront and follow a footpath there, picking up another bus further along the route (the free bus map mentioned below is very detailed and shows such byways and footpaths).

It is possible to return from Hayling to Portsmouth via the north of the island, instead of going back to the ferry.

SOME MORE PLACES TO VISIT For bus times and a free bus guide with map, tel. 0705 696911 or 0705 834769. Buses going inland climb up high hills; those going eastward discover a varied and interesting seashore.

Alexandra Park Leisure Centre (buses no. 7, 8). Indoor and outdoor sports.

+Chichester Harbour (buses no. 302, 702). Alight at Langstone High Street and walk down to waterfront, with old mill, inn and shellfish to buy straight from the sea. Footpath by the sea to Emsworth.

City Museum (buses no. 1, 2, 7, 8, 740 –742, 745–749). Arts and history. Café.

Cumberland House (buses no. 1, 2, 3, 4, 15). Wildlife exhibits and aquarium.

Dickens' birthplace (buses no. 1, 2, 7, 8). Four furnished rooms with some Dickensian mementoes. Oliver Twist pub nearby.

Emsworth Quay (buses no. 329 out and 328 back; or 700). Millpond with swans; sailing-boats; fish can be bought from boats. Lunch at Inn-on-the-Quay.

+Hillsea Lines (many bus services). Old fortifications and zigzag moat now landscaped, with boats, waterfowl, etc. Café.

+Isle of Wight (ferry from harbour, tel. 0705 751751; Hovercraft from Southsea, 0705 829988).

+Leigh Park (buses no. 314, 324). Acres of lawns, lake, gardens (azaleas are superb in May). Farm trail with rare breeds. Café. Good walks in adjoining forest.

+Portchester Castle (bus no. 347). Within colossal Roman walls are a Norman keep and church by the sea. Portchester is a pretty village, with old bakery tearooms and an inn.

+Portsdown and Southwick Hills (buses no. 350, 450). Spectacular views of harbour.

+Queen Elizabeth Country Park (buses no. 748, 749). Downland and forest. Replica of Iron Age farm with demonstrations. Grass skiing and hang-gliding.

+Southwick and Wickham villages, the Meon valley (bus no. 350). A delightful country run. Lunch at Wickham tearooms or wine bar; or picnic in Bere Forest.

+Submarine and submarine museum, Gosport (ferry from The Hard, near coach station).

All the above can be visited nearly every day of the year except for (summer only) the Iron Age farm, Leigh Park farm trail. Harbour or coastal cruises, day-trips to France (for details tel. 0705 822584, 07017 24551, 0705 827701 and 0705 694831).

SOME ANNUAL EVENTS May Crafts Fair. **June** Vintage Vehicles Rally. Fieldgun Displays. Lifeboat Fair. **July** Raft Race. Historic Free Mart Fair. Carnival. **Aug.** Navy Days (dockyard and ships open). Southsea Show (riding, etc.). **Sept.** Searchlight Tattoo, fair on sailing-ship *Foudroyant.*

TOURIST INFORMATION CENTRE Castle Buildings, Clarence Esplanade, Southsea (0705 826722)

Publications obtainable from the Centre include: large, colourful guide with map and accommodation details (50p); mini-guide (free); lists of events, museums and museum events, guided walks, restaurants – all free; Portsmouth Point trail (10p); Owen's Southsea trail (10p); Tudor News (about the *Mary Rose*, 20p); Historic Portsmouth (45p); Fortifications of Old Portsmouth (40p); Natural History of the Portsmouth Area (30p).

The Centre has times of free guided walks, bus tours and coach excursions. Also overnight ferries to Guernsey for duty-free shopping spree.

ECONOMY TIPS Accommodation Packages that include reduced-price coach tours with hotel bookings (0705 696911) and reduced-priced holidays for pensioners. Off-season bargain breaks (0705 826722). **Transport** A travel-card valid for a week gives unlimited bus and train travel over a wide area, covering all the places I've described above (tel. 0705 696911). Day Explorer tickets (see p. 206) take you further afield: Southampton, Chichester, Worthing, Arundel, Midhurst, Singleton and Uppark, for instance. **Admissions** Of the sights I have described, the following are free: HMS *Victory*, Royal Marines Museum, Old Portsmouth, Queen Elizabeth Country Park, Hillsea Lines, Leigh Park Pensioners, children, students and families are entitled to reductions at some others. The Explorer ticket entitles you to 20–50p off entrance fees to various places.

EARLY-CLOSING DAY Wednesday.

LOCAL ALE Gales, Pompey Royal and Strongs.

TO SALISBURY
From London

Coaches depart approximately 4 times a day and the journey takes 2¾ hours (or more, depending upon the route). It passes through hills to Salisbury Plain's vast expanse, with fine views stretching for miles.

Leaving London through Chelsea and Chiswick is a slow but quite interesting start to the journey. Past antique shops and bistros and along Royal Hospital Road there are Wren's buildings for the Chelsea Pensioners who still wear 18th-century uniform (in the graveyard is the tomb of a sergeant who, only at burial, was discovered to be a woman) and the National Army Museum. Lilac and a spectacular wistaria made the scene colourful as we drove along the embankment of the Thames, to our right the tulip gardens, statues, 15th-century Crosby Hall and Georgian terraces of famous Cheyne Walk. It possibly has more blue plaques than any other road in London, showing which houses were once the homes of Carlyle, Hilaire Belloc, Wilson Steer and many other literary or artistic figures – the houses are dotted with commemorative plaques. The two Thames bridges along this stretch of the river are iron ones, decoratively painted, Chelesea Bridge and Albert Bridge. At the point where the colony of houseboats is moored (homes of actors and writers), the coach left the river to inch its way through seedy streets of once fine houses, pillared and balconied, that have suffered decades of neglect. Once past Earls Court we sped across the flyover, Hammersmith's rooftops below us; and then, with glimpses of the Thames in view again, continued by the riverside gardens and old houses of Chiswick – passing Fullers' historic brewery on the left and then, seen through its large gateway, the little classical mansion of Chiswick House on the right, built in 1720 as a replica of Palladio's Villa Capra in Italy.

.

One vast sportsfield after another followed until we crossed the river first at Mortlake (where old inns stand on the waterfront) and then at Twickenham (a lovely view here, of small craft and a fine stone bridge further downriver). The next stretch of the journey would have been unappealing (nothing but suburban semi's for miles) but that I was travelling in May and the road was lined with huge chestnut trees in full flower – first white and then the splendour of the pink ones. We passed a reservoir with a large early Victorian pump house showing how utilitarian building *can* be designed, by contrast with the dreary factories which were then to follow.

Gravel-pit lakes had attracted ducks and, at Thorpe Park (where there are acres of them), a developer who has created a leisure complex – with water sports, replicas of historic ships and dozens of other jollities.

Woodland was succeeded by fields then heaths bright with gorse. All the trees, bare last month, seemed suddenly to have switched on their spring colours. On young Scots pines the new yellow fircones (the male ones) were standing up conspicuously, like candles.

Once we were into Hampshire, the road ran fast and smooth – we skimmed past lush fields and lofty trees, a clear sky with gliders making the most of the breezes (there were several more gliding clubs further along this route).

A brief detour was made to pick up passengers from Basingstoke (very modern office blocks looming over a small park) before pressing on again. Cuttings through the chalk hills speed up the traffic's progress but they cut off the view, and we saw more white gashes being hewn out, for a new motorway. But before long, the coach turned onto an older road where trees met overhead and there were streams fringed by willows.

Another detour took us into the attractive old town of Andover, for a ¼-hour pause to take refreshments. The bus drew up right by the clear, shallow river – every pebble and every strand of bright green waterweed reflecting the sun. I spent the time strolling in the High Street – made wide to accommodate the market – in which on 28 June 1887 Victoria's jubilee was celebrated with a dinner for 5,000 people, seated under decorations and illuminations. These details are recorded beneath dolphins on the blue-and-gold lamppost which stands at the head of the street. Between it and the 1825 Guildhall behind is a circular concourse made of flints decoratively arranged – its date, 1855, embedded in the middle. The citizens of Andover seem to have a passion for dates – they appear on many buildings, particularly the coaching inns: the Globe (its courtyard for coaches now used for antiques) dates from 1742, but the George from 1586. The doorway of the White Hart proclaims that Charles I stayed there several times during the Civil War. In a town like this it is always rewarding to look up, ignoring the 'special offer' placards and other razzmatazz of the shop-fronts, to see the fine upper stories and old roofs above.

We left Andover via a road of sedate Victorian mansions

keeping a seemly distance in their grounds, to return to a landscape of fields and occasional woods. The route runs along the top of a ridge and so there were often magnificent views over the hedges at both sides, well seen through the wide windows of the high coach. We passed small wayside inns and the first thatched houses of the journey.

The coach purred steadily along (a dawdling van in front made speed impossible). The gently rolling hills, cows slowly fording a stream, the acres of tranquil green (which visiting Australians always envy so much!): all combined to make this a very relaxing stretch of the journey.

We crossed the boundary into Wiltshire and could see ahead the hills and clumps of trees which mark the beginning of Salisbury Plain. The onward road switchbacked up and down, and the views stretched even further to the distant horizons, a patchwork of fields (some brilliant with crops of yellow rape) with hills beyond.

A tinkling stream and old stone bridge marked the arrival of Amesbury: many flint walls, greens and Antrobus House, a Georgian mansion which now houses a museum. Fields then became huge: bigger even than the airfield or the golf course that lie among them. This is the edge of Salisbury Plain.

Just after we crossed Salisbury's city boundary, we passed a sign pointing to Old Sarum on the right. Officially Salisbury is still known as New Sarum, the name given to it when Old Sarum, the original city, was abandoned and the new one begun (of which more later). The famous 500-ft spire of Salisbury Cathedral kept appearing and disappearing behind rooftops. We drove by a park, almshouses, dusty Georgian terraces and the library (housed behind the striking façade of what was once the city's market hall), and the half-timbered Chough Hotel. In the big Market Square, stallholders were beginning to pack up their wares for the day. And then we had arrived. The coach stopped in the bus station, with a Tourist Information Centre conveniently adjoining it.

New Sarum, Seven Centuries Old

I sometimes have Australian visitors at my home who, accustomed to cities that are built in orderly style (space being no problem), say it's impossible to find their way around our higgledy-piggledy mediaeval towns, straggling down the hills on which castles were built or squeezed inside city walls, a honeycomb of courts and alleys. They should go to Salisbury where the streets are laid out as squarely as a chessboard – thanks to a 12th-century quarrel between church and king.

The original town was elsewhere, on the windy hill now known as Old Sarum (where ruins of the Norman castle and cathedral still stand, on a site occupied as far back as the Iron Age). The castle, originally built by Bishop Roger early in the 12th century, was soon afterwards annexed by King Stephen (who flung Roger into one of his dungeons to die), which led to such endless strife that eventually the clergy decided to move away from the hill and build a new cathedral elsewhere – in a fertile valley within a loop of the River Avon. Around this a new city quickly developed, an early example of town-planning. The streets were laid out in a grid, and the squares thus formed were often named Chequer this and Chequer that – names still used today. So New Sarum (as the city is still officially called) is simple to explore.

Nearly a hundred mediaeval houses have survived, though to identify them one may have to look above the frontage of a coffee-bar or souvenir shop to spot the telltale mullioned windows or jetted beams of the floor above. The best starting point is the great Market Square (near the bus station in Endless Street), with the architecture most conveniently seen on any day but Tuesday or Saturday when the whole area is seething with market stalls and crowds.

As I looked around the Square, a brewer's dray drawn by great shire horses was delivering kegs to one of the many old inns with latticed bay windows. The Square is surrounded by buildings of great variety, some half-timbered and some Georgian, painted or tile-hung, the skyline made pleasingly irregular by gables and dormers. Near the old Court House, with huge portico and walls of rusticated stone, are shops of quality. The most celebrated one is known as the House of John A'Port, at Three Lion Chequer. Although this is now a large (and varied) china shop, sightseers are welcome to explore its 15th-century rooms. Some of the upper ones have fine panelling or cornices added in the 17th century. Above a fireplace are carved Isaac being sacrified and St Martha (patron saint of cooks). In a much older room, the ancient wattle-and-daub construction of the walls is exposed to view, together with the great hammerbeams of the roof and the clover-leaf outlet for smoke before chimneys were invented.

From an upper window, I could see the lanes that had gradually been built where once only market stalls lined up, in ranks of various specialities: Fish Row, Butcher Row, Oatmeal Row, Ox Row and Silver Street.

I walked via Fish Row to New Canal (the name refers to the channel which, in this as in other streets, once ran alongside the road to provide the citizens with water). Here stands the most unusual cinema in England – fake Gothic outside but the real thing within. Its foyer has a sumptuous roof with angels and a stone fireplace painted in its original colours. This was once the home of a wealthy mayor, Halle, who started the china shop I had just visited and a 'dogge hall' (warehouse for pots and pans), among his other enterprises such as exporting wool and importing wine. Pugin had much to do with the restoration of his stone hall, adding a fancifully carved screen and stained-glass windows with Halle's coat-of-arms.

New Canal Street is where the horse-drawn carts from villages always parked, and still on market days the buses from outlying villages line up here – carriers of people, goods and the week's gossip.

A little further, beyond the 14th-century poultry cross and the half-timbered houses of Silver Street, I found an old watermill, flint-walled, beside its fast-flowing leat where swans and mallards dabble among the green weed. There were young on nests below walls draped in purple toadflax, unperturbed by shoppers hurrying over a small bridge where once a railway line went right into the nearby market hall (now the library). This was the market which features in Hardy's *Jude the Obscure.*

St Thomas's Church (near the mill) is in the book too. Here is another fine angel roof, part of it painted and gilded as it was when new; and a 15th-century 'doom' painting of heaven and hell, with Christ seated on two rainbows. I spotted a king and a bishop both being pushed into the jaws of hell – perhaps a comment by the populace on the unpopularity of both in a town so constantly riven by disputes between Crown and Church. There were finely carved tombstones of slate underfoot, a grand chapel with much woodcarving, stone angels playing musical instruments, a curious holder for the mayoral mace – both the lion and the unicorn being double-headed – and much more.

The 15th-century jacks beneath the clock were striking the hour as I turned away to walk towards the cathedral, wandering along the High Street – past old assembly rooms with cupola, bookshops, the National Trust's House of Steps, a pilgrims' hostel and finally the handsome gateway in the wall that firmly separated secular Salisbury from the cathedral and its precincts. The gate is still locked at night, as in the days when the bishops lived in a state of hostility with the citizenry, or in fear of catching the plagues that regularly decimated the city in the Middle Ages.

I had had only a taste of Salisbury's town life. There are many other streets to explore, with old inns and the meeting places of guilds, more churches, the modern playhouse, an arts centre (with brass-rubbing room), 14th-century almshouses, many waterside meadows or gardens, and the old town gaol underneath the Victorian clock-tower. Salisbury has, of course, its local museum (in The Close) with, among more celebrated items, a room containing the 'drains collection'. This unappealing description covers a multitude of objects retrieved when piped water was laid on and the filthy, typhoid-infested water-channels in the roads drained and filled in: unconsidered trifles from the daily life of nearly seven centuries.

The Cathedral that Constable Loved

Salisbury Cathedral's spire is high and its green close enormous: a picture familiar all the world over from countless chocolate-box and calendar reproductions of Constable's paintings of it. But not even this plethora of cheap reproductions can detract from the tremendous effect made by the famous scene as one walks slowly towards it.

The way to the cathedral lies past Wren's Matrons' College (almshouses) and Choristers' Green, surrounded by historic buildings where wistaria and magnolia drape themselves on mellow brick walls and the lead rainwater-heads declare their age (1701). Mompesson House belongs to the National Trust and is open to the public. The great Close, too, is surrounded by fine buildings, mostly mediaeval or Georgian; with, a modern touch, Elisabeth Frink's 'Walking Madonna' in bronze standing in the middle of the lawns.

After so much rambling, I was glad of a coffee in the cathedral's former 'plumbery' (workshop for the plumbers who looked after the lead roof). The café is manned by a rota of volunteers from neighbouring parishes, who bring in homemade food ('church mouse' lunches of soup and cheese were on offer at 75p) to eat at chunky tables made from the Close's fallen elms. The cathedral guides, too, are volunteers – they will take you up to the spire if you have a head for this, scrambling among the 14th-century internal scaffolding on which it is built.

Unlike many, this cathedral is all of one style inside, having been built in its entirety between 1220 and 1258. Recently its somewhat austere interior has been given a focal-point of blue (particularly vivid in early morning) by the 'Prisoners of Conscience' window over the altar – made in Chartres. You really need binoculars to identify in the complex abstract design all the familiar images of Christ's suffering, the identifiable portraits of some prisoners of conscience today, and symbols such as barbed wire and bars or the star of hope and the anchor of faith. Nearby is a 17th-century verse of George Herbert:

A man that looks on glass
On it may stay his eye;
Or, if it pleaseth, through it pass
And then the heaven espy.

As I entered, the 14th-century 'bishop's bell', the oldest working clock in the world, was striking, its visible mechanism attracting a group of spectators. I lingered at the many magnificent tombs in the cathedral (an early one of William Longespee, bastard brother of King John, is of special interest: dressed in chain mail, he lies with a long shield decorated with lions, the first known use of these as an emblem of English royalty); gazed up at the soaring Perpendicular arches that were added to strengthen the crossing when the 6,000-ton spire above was built in the 14th century; and at the marvel of the fan-vaulting in one of the chapels. Salisbury has the largest cloisters of any cathedral, with two immense cedars spreading their branches wide in the middle of them; and an octagonal chapter house with 13th-century figures from the Bible all round it. On a stone bench some mediaeval hand had incised the layout for a board game: a detail that William Golding (once a local teacher) noticed and used in his novel *The Spire*. He described how Jocelin, high up in the half-built tower, realised with horror that the wind was swaying it – because part of the board game scratched in a stone bench below moved in and out of view as he gazed down.

The famous library, started in 1089, was closed when I was there but a few of its treasures were on display including one of the only three copies of Magna Carta to have survived for nearly eight centuries – all 3,500 words exquisitely written on a single parchment.

Despite its unique treasures, the interior of the cathedral is, to my mind, outshone by its exterior. The superb building is not hemmed in, like so many cathedrals, by houses crowding round it like chickens under a hen: the early bishops, when they designed their New Sarum, kept the plebs at a respectful distance outside the walled precincts. As a result, the great building stands in splendid isolation, a jewel lying on the green velvet of the surrounding lawns.

SOME MORE PLACES TO VISIT For bus times and route maps, tel. 0722 6855. Also Around Salisbury by Bus. Routes to the north cross Salisbury Plain. Others wind among downs or follow streams, passing through old villages.

Amesbury (buses no. 202, 203, 205, 206, 208, 209). Church, river with small weir, coaching inns, market, museum.

Breamore House (buses no. X3, 238, 240). Bus follows main Bournemouth road, through villages of half-timbered and thatched houses. The Elizabethan mansion is ½ mile from Breamore village: it contains paintings, etc., carriage museum and countryside museum.

+Downton (buses no. X3, 238, 240; or, better, 243–5). Very picturesque waterside village, among downs. Plenty of attractive walks nearby. Inns, etc. Cuckoo Fair in May.

+Figsbury Ring (buses no. 276, 277, 280). Route follows a main road; then a steep walk to hilltop with spectacular views. Earth ramparts of 15-acre Iron Age fort at top (National Trust).

+Fordingbridge (buses no. X3, 238). Beyond Breamore, see above. At far end are streams, old church, park and footpaths. Plenty of restaurants and small shops. Albany Hotel has riverside terrace.

+Harnham Mill (bus no. 255). Overlooking stream and water meadows painted by Constable. Part of the watermill is Saxon; café and crafts inside. One can stroll back to Salisbury across the meadows.

+Old Sarum (buses no. 202, 203, 205, 206, 208, 209). An uphill walk, worth the effort, to a sunny but windswept height, with huge Norman castle ruins. Lunch at Old Castle Inn, by bus stop. One can walk back to Salisbury by riverside path.

Rockbourne Roman Villa (buses no. X3, 238 to Fordingbridge, then no. 242). Seventy rooms have been excavated. With museum.

St Martin's (buses no. 36, 37, X7). Very ancient church on the outskirts of Salisbury (ribbed timber roof). Nearby are the many acres of Winston Churchill gardens, with a network of rivers.

Shaftesbury (buses no. 226–8). Hilltop town with abbey, etc. A scenic route.

+Stonehenge (buses no. 200, 203). England's biggest bore, if you ask me; but millions choose to visit it.

Tilshead (buses no. 270, 271, 272). Route with views of Salisbury Plain, its villages and streams.

Wilton (buses no. 225–8, 260, 261). Historic small town with carpet factory – morning tours. Sheep Fair, mediaeval stained glass in the church, several inns, etc.

+Wilton House and grounds (buses no. 225–8, 260, 261). Outstanding 17th-century mansion with world-famous paintings and antiques. Adventure playground. 7,000 model soldiers in battle array. Crafts. Excellent café. Frequent events (e.g. flower show).

All the above can be visited nearly every day of the year except for some that close in winter: Breamore House, Wilton House, Regimental Museum.

SOME ANNUAL EVENTS April Folk Festival. **May** Craft Fair. Maypole Dancing. Veteran Car Rally. **June** Carnival Fête. Mayor-making ceremonial. **July** Southern Cathedrals Festival (every third year). **Sept.** Salisbury Festival. **Oct.** Charter Fair. **Nov.** Advent Carols at the cathedral. **Dec.** Christmas Carols. Boxing Day meet in Guildhall Square.

TOURIST INFORMATION CENTRES
10 Endless Street (0722 4956)
City Hall, Fisherton Street (0722 27676)
Publications obtainable from the Centres include: Salisbury and the Heart of Wessex, guidebook with maps and gazetteer (70p); Mini-guide, with street plan (10p); street plan (free); Town Trail (free); What's On, monthly (free); Real Ale Guide to pubs in Salisbury and south Wiltshire (20p); Local Walks, pack of 6 (35p).

The Centres have information about guided walks of the town (by day or in the evening when floodlighting is on), cathedral guides, private guides for hire, guided coach tours and cycle hire. It is possible to have a 'Hardy' or a 'Constable' tour. Leaflet about a circular bus tour is available (Marlborough, Avebury, Devizes).

ECONOMY TIPS Accommodation
Youth Hostel: Millford Hill House, Milford Hill (tel. 0722 27572). **Transport**
Getaway tickets provide unlimited bus travel for a day; day returns are cheaper than two singles; and Bus-about tickets give a week's unlimited travel.

Explorer tickets (see p. 206) can be used to go to Bath, Aldershot (military museums), Marlborough, Winchester, Chawton (Jane Austen's home), Southampton, Portsmouth, Marwell Park (wildlife), Beaulieu, New Forest, Lymington, Bournemouth. Poole, Swanage, Wareham, Corfe Castle, Weymouth, Dorchester. **Admissions** Explorer ticket entitles holder to reductions at some places.

EARLY-CLOSING DAY Wednesday

MARKET DAYS Tuesdays and Saturdays. (As well as general market in the square, there are antiques markets in the town mill and in Fisherton Street.) Cattle market on Tuesdays.

LOCAL ALE Gibbs.

TO SHERBORNE
From Salisbury

Coaches depart twice a day and the journey takes about 1¼
hours. It goes through very beautiful countryside with varied
views of hills, villages and river valleys. A good stop on the way
would be the ancient, hilltop town of Shaftesbury.

The coach arrived within minutes at Wilton House and the pretty
little town of Wilton (see p. 137) where a stream trickles by the
roadside, there are lanes of colourwashed houses and pollarded
limes stand on the green. A lot of houses along the start of this route
combine flints with brick, in chequerboard or banded patterns, but
later there were cottages of half-timbering and thatch or fine stone
houses. The River Nadder stayed with us for a while, and across its
valley I could see hills with military badges cut into the chalk
(mementoes of the First World War) and a huge map of Australia.

This is a rural route, far from any motorway, with peaceful
scenes as we passed by – brown hens scratching in an orchard, swan
with cygnets on a lake, creeper-covered inns, old cottages half
hidden behind fruit blossom, and trout streams sparkling in the
sunshine. The road winds up and down, eventually making the
climb up to Shaftesbury, an old market town perched on a hilltop.

The road into the town is lined with old stone cottages, and the
coach paused to pick up passengers right outside the 13th-century
church, its walls of soft stone weather-worn and much in need of
restoration. Shaftesbury has a castellated town hall, secretive alleyways, pillared coaching inn and old cobbled courtyards. To the
abbey used to come pilgrims seeking the shrine of St Edward, the
martyr king who was murdered at Corfe in 978. Little remains of the
abbey, except for a few finds in the town museum – including what
may be Edward's bones, in a lead box. The Grosvenor Hotel is

worth a visit to see the great, carved 'Chevy Chase' sideboard.

As we turned out of the town and started downhill, I glanced backward for a spectacular view – mile upon mile of plains, fields and hills stretching into the distance.

The rest of the journey continued as before, with many streams to cross, verges occasionally colourful with campions and bluebells, and great old barns – their slate roofs gilded with lichen, soon to arrive at Sherborne, one of England's most beautiful yet least publicised ancient towns.

The Church that was Once an Abbey

The coach drops one off at The Green, itself an attractive spot with Tudor houses close by, from which it is only a short walk to reach the famous Abbey. Strolling down Cheap Street, one passes mediaeval and Georgian buildings (many with bow windows or timber framing) and the entrance to Swan Yard which won a conservation award for its conversion from stables to a little shopping precinct, lined with antique and craft shops. Because, here and elsewhere, there is a story to many of Sherborne's houses, it is particularly worth getting the 'Town Walk' leaflet (listed below) before arriving – it tells you about the literary or other associations, and inside which shops you can discover such things as a painted ceiling depicting the four seasons.

At the bottom of the street is the Tudor 'conduit' (the decorative little building where the monks used to wash); and down tiny Church Lane nearby is the excellent local museum – well worth an unhurried visit.

But it is, of course, the great abbey church which is the centrepiece of Sherborne. Its stonework, which has only recently been cleaned and restored, seemed to glow in the morning sun and I needed no guidebook to assure me that this is unquestionably one of the most beautiful churches in England. Its great interior is equal in splendour, with some of the finest fan-vaulting in the country. The elaborately carved bosses in the roof have been restored too, and are now brilliantly coloured and gilded. Some of the fan-vaults are nearly 30 feet wide. As to their bosses, there are over a hundred in the nave alone – so detailed that every feather or leaf or petal is individually carved. In complete contrast is the reredos of shining glass engraved by Laurence Whistler in 1968, with symbols of glory and fruitfulness.

The precincts, too, deserve a visit, and I threaded my way amongst the twists and turns of the old walls to emerge among the buildings of Sherborne School – a monastic school until Henry VIII closed it when he turned the monks out of their Abbey in 1539 . It was re-founded, as a grammar school, by his son Edward VI.

Two Castles

The Old Castle was built in the 12th century by the great Bishop Roger of Salisbury, second only to Henry I in power and prestige (see p. 132), who was also Abbot of Sherborne. The New Castle was begun by Sir Walter Raleigh in 1594. Although both can be reached from the Abbey by walking up Long Street, which has some historic houses, it is easier to take a bus (no. 468–9 or 470 from Greenhill) to the Black Horse inn.

The Old Castle's ruins are perched on a hilltop: a windswept and romantic site, worth the steep walk. As at Old Sarum, the castle was seized by Stephen but later reverted to the bishops, who then used it as a residence. It was reduced to ruins by the Parliamentarians during the Civil War.

At its foot is the village of Castleton (= castle town), with an unusual little Georgian church and houses. In the church is a memorial to the old lady who gave money to build it: for 70 years, a domestic servant at the New Castle in the service of the Digby family, who still live there.

This Castle is in complete contrast to the dramatic ruins on the hill – although it, too, is a fine sight from a distance, with towers, chimneys and stone beasts creating a memorable silhouette. It stands in a park (landscaped by Capability Brown) so huge that a small map is provided for those who want to explore its copses and pleasure-grounds, lake, orangery, Roman mosaic, rare trees, tearoom and so forth. The house itself is full of treasures from four centuries – the hall is Elizabethan, the oak room Jacobean, the library Georgian and the solarium Victorian.

Sherborne deserves a long visit because, in addition to its abbey and these two castles, there are a great many minor buildings of interest, too numerous to describe in this chapter. It stands comparison with many old cathedral cities and, like them, is well supplied with good eating-places, antique and craft shops. And because it has eleven schools, there are plenty of bookshops and cultural events (it is the home of the Dorset Opera Company).

SOME MORE PLACES TO VISIT For bus timetable with route map, tel. 0935 6233. This area is not well supplied by buses, but such routes as exist are through very beautiful countryside.
+Compton House (buses no. 468, 469). Worldwide Butterflies now occupies this stately home (and grounds): a unique living museum of butterflies, and of silkworms. Café. Really outstanding, it needs at least half a day.
Nether Compton (bus no. 470). A roundabout ride westward to Yeovil, winding among fine gardens and old houses.
Oborne and Poyntington (bus no. 470). A pretty route eastwards, worth taking just for the ride: streams, thatched cottages, wildflowers, views and downs.
Purse Caundle Manor (buses no. 468, 469). Mediaeval mansion, still occupied, with walled garden, beyond a village with stream. Nearby Venn Garden Centre has glasshouses of orchids.

Except for the Museum, all places described close in the winter.

SOME ANNUAL EVENTS April Blessing Paschal candles at the Abbey. **May** Horse trials (at the Castle). **Aug.** Carnival. **Oct.** Teddy Roe's Band heralds in the Pack Monday Fair. (Teddy Roe's Band is a traditional midnight frolic with klaxons and tin drums.) **Dec.** Christingle and carols at the Abbey.

TOURIST INFORMATION CENTRE
Hound Street (093581 5341)
Publications obtainable from the Centre include a free pack containing the following leaflets: Welcome to Sherborne (with street plan); Town Walk; Antiques Guide; Accommodation; Restaurants; Walks in the Country; Hardy Country.
The Centre has information about coach excursions.

ECONOMY TIPS Accommodation There are bargain breaks at the Post House Hotel. **Transport** There are Rambler tickets for a week's unlimited bussing in Dorset and Somerset. Set-Farer is for a dozen journeys at a discount; Day-Farers are cheap day returns; Welfarer provides half-price travel for pensioners: all these three are valid throughout the west country.

EARLY-CLOSING DAY Wednesday.

MARKET DAYS Thursdays and Saturdays.

LOCAL ALE & FOOD Huntsman ale. Blue Vinney cheese. Dorset knobs (biscuits).

TO SHREWSBURY
From Worcester

Coaches depart daily, and the journey takes about 1½ hours. It goes through some of the most outstanding scenery in England. A good stop on the way would be Bridgnorth, with historic houses, caves and a Norman tower that leans more than Pisa's (unless you prefer to pause at Kidderminster to look for carpet bargains).

It took a bit of slow huffing and puffing to edge our way through the brick-and-privet suburbs of Worcester, past Barbourne Park and out to where fields of vegetables stretched towards a horizon of sharp-peaked hills. There were occasional black-and-white farmhouses in the middle distance, ponds green with weed, and 'pick your own' fields where stout, pink-faced ladies bent double to gather their strawberries. The road curved its way through the hills, sometimes hemmed in by tall hedges that brushed the coach windows, or powdered with a shower of blossom falling from tall trees. Here and there the earth showed reddish – almost the colour of carrot soup.

Kidderminster is not a town that aims to please: its outskirts are a squalid jostle of carpet factories and car parks, with no attempt at orderly layout or screening from view. We paused within a canyon-like street between grimy brick factories of Victorian vintage before pressing on past gasometers (and past the office of estate agents named as Doolittle and Dalley: now *there's* honesty in advertising!).

The scenery improved after that – marguerites crowding the verges, bright green bracken spreading up the hillsides. Sometimes the view was shut off as we went through deep cuttings in the hills, and then suddenly a vast panorama would spring into sight. The summer grass was so tall that lambs lay half-hidden in it, little black heads raised in curiosity to watch us speed by. Black hens scratched

in a dusty farmyard, cows sought the shade under spreading oaks. A number of inns round here are called the Royal Oak, for this is Civil War country where the story of Charles' hiding-place in an oak tree is still retold.

Our road twisted and turned, swaying the passengers in the coach. The remaining stretch of the journey has some of the most beautiful scenery of any routes described in this book, and with great variety. We passed a lake in a valley, Dudmaston (a National Trust property), a pine forest, the calm and shining River Severn, red sandstone cliffs by the road and then the old town of Bridgnorth.

This is one of England's two-level towns – the upper half is perched on a clifftop, with a cliff-side railway to lower foot-passengers to the part below. We entered Bridgnorth through the low town. It was a squeeze to get in past the terraced cottages, lopsided little black-and-white houses, small antique shops and mediaeval inns, all crammed together – with inn signs and hanging flower baskets adding colourful touches to the scene. We crossed the river, where boys were fishing from grassy banks, in order to make our way to the upper (Georgian) town along a road of serpentine bends. In the red cliffs were doors where cellars had been gouged out. Colourful vetch and clover sprawled by the wayside, garden roses and mock orange blossom scented the warm air as we reached the top.

Out among the fields, a light breeze riffled through the wheat, giving it the appearance of shot silk; and the far hills, half lost in a haze of heat, seemed like a pile of soft blue pillows. There were villages of sandstone houses, occasional magnificent gateways or glimpses of stately homes, and always, beyond the lush grass or the fields of grain, a vast unspoilt landscape spreading over hundreds of acres – a succession of views of incomparable beauty, for mile after mile.

We were high up, among big fields already turning to a ripe gold, bordered by beech hedges or others where briar roses rambled at will. In one field, hundreds of poppies spread in a great scarlet swathe through a field of wheat. In another, two farm labourers – mahogany faces shining with sweat – heaved bales of hay into a stack. At Much Wenlock, there were half-timbered houses and drystone walls.

Shrewsbury announced itself with a dramatic exclamation mark: a 130-foot column (to the memory of Lord Hill, Wellington's second-in-command at Waterloo), which stands high above the town centre. The coach sped swiftly down from here, passing what is left of the abbey (red stone walls contrasting with green grass) and then across one of the ten bridges that give access to the old town, which stands on what is virtually an island – for Shrewsbury was built within a horseshoe bend of the River Severn, which encircles it almost like a moat.

We swept round the south-east perimeter – following the line of the old town walls. Unlike car drivers, we could see over the top and look down to the lawns and gardens below, and over rooftops. To the right stands a most unusual church, St Chad's: a classical building with a round nave. And then we had arrived – drawing up right in the centre of the town and beside one of its treasures, the huge Tudor mansion, now a museum of local history, known as Rowley's House.

Mediaeval Market Town

The old town of half-timbered houses and inns is compact, confined to the top of the mound around which the River Severn forms a natural moat (except for the north side, where a Norman castle, largely rebuilt by Edward I, guards the landward approach). This makes it ideal to explore on foot all the alleys, byways and old houses galore which are what, collectively, give Shrewsbury so much character. No grand vistas or towering cathedral here: instead, the town has an intimate character. Its oddly angled streets (with such names as Dogpole, Wyle Cop, Coffeehouse Passage, Shoplatch and Water Lane) still follow the mediaeval plan – or lack of plan. A street map is essential.

Right in the centre is The Square, a good starting point and, like other Shrewsbury streets, full of hanging flower baskets during summer. The open-pillared Old Market Hall, built in the reign of Elizabeth I and embellished with carved figures, is sometimes still used for its original purpose: when I was there, a 'flea market' was doing a busy trade, well protected from the rain that suddenly poured down. The square is a medley of architectural styles: for example, an early Victorian music hall now houses the Tourist Information Centre, Woolley's House dates from Queen Anne's reign and the Plough Inn is largely Tudor. Banks and shops occupy what were once wool merchants' houses, their half-timbered façades ornate with carved mouldings, warriors and suchlike.

I left the square to make my way up the steep and narrow slit of Grope Lane, the leaden sky scarcly visible between the overhanging upper storeys (no need to explain why this alley got its name). At the top are Bear Steps, with a 14th-century hall now restored to its former glory, along with an arcade of little shops adjoining it. The Civic Society often have interesting exhibitions here, and there is a café. This was a quiet spot, adjoining the churchyard of St Alkmund, where the loudest sound was the chirping of sparrows and the splash of rain.

Another narrow alley led past Prince Rupert's Hotel (it, too, started life as the mansion of a Tudor cloth merchant) to St Mary's Church, a red sandstone building standing on a green. Its interior is particularly colourful – the rugged stone walls mottled in pale or pinkish colours (the overall effect is pearly) and light entering through the rich and rare Jesse window, as detailed as a tapestry, with over four dozen biblical personages depicted in rows – 14th-century work. The roof is full of carved flowers and fruit. Eight heraldic angels spread their wings wide. Even the tiled floor is colourful. An electric polisher hummed and there was a smell of Brasso in the air as pinafored ladies busied themselves among all this glory. This fine church stands in the district where most of the Tudor cloth merchants lived, and just outside is their Drapers' Hall, a fine example of timber framing in Shrewsbury style – quatrefoils in the main timbers, and cable-like carving.

I walked round the back of the church and past the huge Greek portico of the Royal Salop Infirmary which, founded in 1747, was one of the first public hospitals in Britain, but is now full of luxury flats. From here, Dogpole led downhill, past more black-and-white buildings, the classical Guildhall – cheerful with fuchsias and geraniums, an Italianate tabernacle (now a 'pot shop' which attracts bargain-hunters), the Olde House of herringbone brickwork between timber framing, and many big arches for coaches with views beyond. Dogpole Court was particularly attractive – brick paving, baskets of flowers and shining brass doorknockers.

The narrow alleys which in Plymouth are called 'opes' in Shrewsbury are called 'shuts': now what may *that* suggest about the psychological outlook of their respective inhabitants, I wondered, as I turned up the winding thoroughfare of Wyle Cop (Welsh for hilltop) to look for St Julian's.

This disused church is now a crafts centre, with booths for leatherworkers, jewellers, knitters, enamellers and so on – making and selling their wares in the odour of sanctity. The marble pulpit wore a rakish signboard, 'To the restaurant'.

I had loitered my time away, and had seen only a little of what Shrewsbury has to offer. There was time only to go (via the house where Clive of India lived as Shrewsbury's MP, 1761–74, now a museum with a good china collection) for a stroll in the Quarry Gardens, between the town walls and the river. Percy Thrower used to be in charge here and it was he who, in 1946, designed the colourful flower gardens of The Dingle. Beyond these I found the Shoemakers' Arbour, half hidden by the flowers of a climbing hydrangea, and beyond this some rather charming godwottery of rusticwork. The arbour is the only one to survive out of dozens erected by the various trade guilds of the town.

There was a great deal more that I had barely glimpsed: the Georgian quarter, for instance, as well as many other mediaeval streets, no less than five military museums and the arts centre. But there was only time to slip into the covered market for a punnet of strawberries before running to catch my homeward-bound coach.

SOME MORE PLACES TO VISIT For bus times and route maps, tel. 0743 62485. Particularly helpful for weekenders is the booklet Which Sunday Service? (10p). Bus routes go through lush farming country and famous hill scenery, with woods and rivers along the way. Very good walking country: the bus company has produced a guide to seven walks in the Wrekin area (35p).

+**Atcham** (buses no. X96, 892, 893). Attingham Park (National Trust): opulent Georgian mansion, park by Repton, riverside walk. Café.

Battlefield (buses no. X64, 928, 929). Where the Battle of Shrewsbury took place in 1403, a fine church was built to commemorate it.

Broseley (bus no. X96 to Ironbridge, then no. 9). Clay pipe factory. Benthall Hall (National Trust).

+**Buildwas** (bus no. X96). Norman abbey ruins and nature trail.

Cardington and Condover (buses no. 955, 956). Stone village and Condover Hall: Elizabethan mansion, open only in August. Nature trail at Condover.

+**Church Stretton** (buses no. 955, 956). Scenic route alongside the Long Mynd: A E. Housman country. Walks by streams in Carding Mill valley (National Trust). Nature trail in Old Rectory Wood. Craft shops. Summer arts festival. Cafés.

Coleham Pumping Station (a few minutes' walk). Museum with two working beam-engines.

Cosford (buses no. 892, 893). Aerospace museum, including NASA moonbuggie.

+**Craven Arms** (buses no. 955, 956). For walks along Wenlock Edge; or – ¾ mile – to Stokesay Castle (13th century, still lived in).

+**Earls Hill Nature Trail** (bus no. 960). ½ mile from Pontesford petrol station. A beautiful and varied mile-long trail rising to over 1,000 ft (but one need not go all the way up).

+**Ellesmere** (bus no. 981). Lakes, wildfowl, watersports, gardens, information centre: 114 acres. Café.

Frankwell Riverside trail (guidebook, 20p, from Tourist Information Centre). Starts on the far side of Shrewsbury's Welsh Bridge.

+**Grinshill** (bus no. 985). Beauty spot.

+**Hodnet Hall** (buses no. X64, 928, 929). 60 acres of landscaped flower gardens, with lakes (café).

Horsehay (bus no. 893). Steam engine centre.

Ironbridge (buses no. X96, 893). A scenic valley route to six square miles of the Severn Gorge with a series of museums, some open-air, devoted to industrial history (coal, iron and china).

+**Leebotwood** and **Woolstaston** (buses no. 955, 956 plus 2-mile walk). Picturesque villages: thatched inn, ancient earthworks, village green, etc.

Lilleshall (bus no. 892 to Wellington, then no. 2). 13th-century abbey.

Longnor (bus no. 955, 956). Longnor Hall, Jacobean mansion. Open · by appointment, tel. 0743 73543.

+**Lyth Hill** (buses no. S17, S19, 955, 956). Mary Webb associations.

Meole Brace (bus no. S6). William Morris's best stained glass in the church. Mary Webb associations.

Moreton Corbet (bus no. X64). 13th-century castle.

+**Much Wenlock** (bus no. 964). Guildhall, priory and museum.

Nesscliffe (bus no. V1). Herb farm.

Percy Thrower's Garden Centre (bus no. S8).

Shifnal (buses no. X96, 892, 893). Fine church in old country town.

+**Uffington** (bus no. 926). Haughmond Abbey ruins.

+**Weston Park** (bus no. X96). 17th-century mansion with outstanding paintings and furniture. Deer park, lake and gardens designed by Capability Brown; as well as playground, aquarium, pony rides, miniature railway, nature trail, etc. Café.

+**Wroxeter** (bus no. X96). Remains of Roman town.

Places mentioned are open on most days throughout the year, except for the following which close in winter: Much Wenlock Guildhall, Stokesay Castle, Attingham Park, Acton Scott Working Farm Museum, Hodnet Hall gardens.

SOME ANNUAL EVENTS May County Agricultural Show. **June** Regatta and Carnival. Hunter Trials. Folk Music Festival. **July** International Youth Music Festival. Raft Race. **Aug.** Flower show (huge). **Oct.** National Ploughing Championships. River Race.

TOURIST INFORMATION CENTRE The Square (0743 52019)
Publications obtainable from the Centre include: Official guide to Shrewsbury and environs – excellent (50p); Mini-guide, with town plan (10p); Buildings of Special Interest (40p); Town centre map (free); Town trail (50p); Nature trails in Shropshire (free); Shrewsbury Castle (10p); The Bridges (2p); Charles Darwin in Shrewsbury (free); Shrewsbury Museums (free); What's On, monthly (free); Accommodation list (free); Nature trails accessible by bus – Preston Montford, Corbet Wood, Grinshill, Merrington Green (15p each).
The Centre has details of free guided walks in the town (and others for countryside, farm or industrial archaeology), coach excursions and cycle hire.

ECONOMY TIPS Accommodation There are bargain breaks, and off-season discounts for pensioners. Youth Hostel: Woodlands, Abbey Foregate. **Transport** Explorer tickets (see p. 206) can be used to visit Telford (vast shopping centre), Bridgnorth (see p. 146), Ludlow (historic town and castle), Ironbridge, etc. In this area, there are particularly good booklets given away with Explorer tickets. **Admissions** Of places mentioned, the following are free: Bear Steps hall, Clive's house, Coleham pumping station, Condover Hall, regimental museums, Rowley's museum, Shrewsbury abbey, Ellesmere mere, Moreton Corbet castle, herb farm at Nesscliffe.

EARLY-CLOSING DAY Thursday.

MARKETS General market: Wednesdays, Fridays and Saturdays. Cattle market: Tuesdays.

LOCAL ALE & FOOD Wem ales. Shrewsbury biscuits.

TO TAUNTON
From Sherborne*

Coaches depart daily and the journey takes 1½ hours. It goes through countryside that is not only varied but often has outstanding views for miles around. A good stop on the way would be Ilminster which has byways, a fine church and old buildings worth exploring.

A fast road sped us to Yeovil after which the journey on to Crewkerne became more attractive. Many cottages in this part of the world are of sandstone, or else colourwashed and thatched, with leaded panes in mullioned windows. The scenery is pastoral, often with great views laid out at one's feet like a map. High hedges enclose rich fields where cows graze.

Down the road swooped, through leafy valleys, and then up once more to the high hilltops with those distant views again (on a clear day, it is said to be possible to see both the Bristol Channel to the north and the English Channel to the south): the name of one, Windwhistle Hill – 750 feet up, tells its own story. The sunlight flickered onto the road wherever there were stretches with trees meeting overhead, and then would follow miles of open country and, at Cricket St Thomas, an avenue of beeches beside the fine park of a thousand acres surrounding the Georgian mansion (and wildlife park) where *To the Manor Born* was filmed. There were flint lodges, handsome gateways, many wayside inns and hedges of holly and laurel along the way.

Chard swiftly came and went: an old lace-making town with a mile-long High Street which has a Tudor courthouse (used by Judge Jeffreys during the 'Bloody Assizes' after Monmouth's rebellion) opposite a very imposing town hall with Doric colonnade astride the pavement and a great clock-tower above, where the coach stopped to pick up passengers. The church is embellished with gargoyles, the

houses with verandahs or bay windows, their stone walls pleasantly varied in colour.

As we continued westward a vast panorama stretched out ahead of the road: a rather bumpy, zigzag road that set all the ashtrays in the coach jingling in anything but unison. Farms looked prosperous, with huge centuries-old barns awaiting the harvest to come. When we turned off towards Ilminster, there were streams threading their way through the fields, willows weeping into them, and a pond of swans and ducks. Ilminster is a low-lying town, once a market for wool, with a Perpendicular church of particular grandeur (housing the Jacobean tomb of the couple who founded Wadham College, Oxford), its pinnacled and crocketed tower soaring high above the grass and tombs of the churchyard. A butter-cross stands in the middle of the small market square. The Ham stone used for the church tower, which is copied from the central tower of Wells cathedral, and for other buildings is very orangey in colour, quarried from Hamdon Hill.

Up and down the road we went, past a field of tethered bulls and others of sheep or wheat, over more streams and by more thatched cottages, until we began to move into cider country and a succession of orchards. Wistaria was coming into blossom against old stone walls, and a group of horse chestnuts standing in a field of buttercups were beautiful to see. The summer sunshine was now streaming in from the west, so I moved over to the shadier side of the coach and opened the overhead ventilators. The traffic was increasing, and already the great tower of Taunton's church was in view. We passed under a flyover and through dreary suburbs – not a good first impression – to draw up right in the middle of the city.

Walks Free of Traffic

A traveller hurrying through Taunton might easily suppose it was not worth a second glance: just a hustling, traffic-laden county town. For Taunton keeps its many charms tucked away behind the main thoroughfares, in parts that the pounding traffic never reaches.

The coach station, however, is ideally placed for discovering many of these secret places: it occupies what was once virtually an island surrounded by marshes, at the very centre of the original Saxon settlement from which the town grew. Right by it is the Winchester Arms with sun umbrellas outside, and there are lawns for picnicking. To one side of it are the remains of the mediaeval castle (now housing the extremely good Somerset County Museum); a short footpath leads to the very lovely lawns and trees bordering the River Tone only a few yards away, well populated with geese and ducks; to the side of the Castle Hotel is flowery and peaceful Norman Garden on the site of the keep; and just across the way are the Municipal Buildings including more parts of the castle (round the other side of which is the Tourist Information Centre). I have yet to find a coach station which has so much of interest all around it, and so many quiet spots close at hand in which to wander or relax.

To explore any further afield than this, it is helpful to have obtained, before arriving, the free town plan (listed below) which shows footpaths as well as roads. With the help of this, it is easy to find the short waterside path that leads north from close by the coach station to French Weir and a little park beyond. Or the one that follows the River Tone east and soon arrives at the bridge from which boat trips start, and at the Brewhouse Theatre and Arts Centre, a very good place to have an inexpensive homemade lunch.

South of the coach station is Bath Place (little more than an alley, but lined with cottages, antique shops and suchlike) at the end of which a stroll southward along the pedestrianised High Street leads one to the colourful great iron gates of Vivary Park. This park (named for the mediaeval vivarium or fishponds which used to be here) stretches a mile out into the countryside. (If you don't want to walk all the way back from the far end, buses can be picked up to take you back to the coach station.) The park has something for everyone – the flowerbeds, fountain and gaily painted bandstand give way to less formal acres, a stream and lake; followed by sportsfields and a children's play area (with a little railway). Overlooking this park are the elegant backs of Regency houses and the exotic red towers of Jellabad Barracks, a masterpiece of elaborately decorative brickwork.

An Award-winning Museum

Collections of pots can be pretty boring: not so at the Somerset County Museum, inside what is left of the castle that was built by King Stephen's brother, partly destroyed by Henry II, rebuilt in Henry III's reign, beseiged in Henry VI's and again in Charles I's. Here Judge Jeffreys sentenced some 500 participants in Monmouth's rebellion of 1685. Where so much violence occurred, all is now serene.

As to the pots, I found them so absorbing that I had scarcely enough time for the other galleries. Here at last were displays that vividly explained the differences of earthenware, stoneware and porcelain, and their glazes. Styles moved on century by century, with examples from sites all over the county. Potters congregated in Crock Street, from a well in which 26 mediaeval water-jugs have been retrieved. There is a case full of puzzle and joke pots, and another of the unique Elton ware made in the 1880s with metallic and crackle effects.

But there is a lot else in this museum. 'And So To Bed' is a still-life of patchwork quilt, nightcap, candle-snuffer and potty. There's a huge collection of horse brasses and bells; an entire military museum upstairs; and down below a 20-foot Iron Age canoe gouged out of a single oak. A huge Roman mosaic of Dido and Aeneas. A Saxon loom recreated from stone weights dug up some years ago. And, a small sensation when it was unearthed in 1980, the Taunton hoard. When Taunton was under attack during the Civil War, some man of wealth hid his all in a clay pot and buried it. He did not survive to retrieve his cache, but over 300 years later it came to light: a treasure trove of 275 silver coins. And another treasure: a 14th-century stone reredos with angels and saints, found (upside down) in use as a floor. From the sublime to the ridiculous: a bar of workhouse soap that has survived the years, albeit chewed by mice; and a moustache cup, shaped to keep those Victorian whiskers out of the tea.

There is even more to Taunton than this. In busy North Street, the Post Office has a Telecommunications Museum which illustrates, with working exhibits, the history of the telephone and telegraph (you can phone a friend via a 1920s switchboard). The whole area behind this street is gradually being restored: alleyways lead to a network of neglected terraces well worth conservation and which will one day be a pleasure to explore. One of the first parts to have been completed is The Courtyard in Middle Street, where a cluster of small craft studios and speciality shops are now trading, with a restaurant. St Mary's church dominates this quarter, set in a peaceful churchyard with yews shading its daisy-filled lawns. Built early in the 17th century, it has the most outstanding Perpendicular tower in Somerset – a county well endowed with such towers. High up inside the church are angels, and an exceptionally fine wooden roof.

In another direction (south of the coach station) is the Georgian part of the town. The Crescent is an impressive and handsome street, comparable with some in Bath. Taunton has Somerset's county cricket ground, too (just beyond the theatre mentioned above), and a huge cattle market. The more energetic can walk twelve miles from the town centre to Bridgwater on the canal towpath and then take a bus back. Altogether, this is a town of great variety, with plenty of pleasant surprises for anyone willing to search them out. And, above all, it is an ideal town for a visitor who arrives without a car.

SOME MORE PLACES TO VISIT Bus rides around Taunton lead to scenic areas with views of hills – the Quantocks to the north, Brendon and Blackdown Hills to west and south. For bus time-table with route map, tel. 0823 72033.
Bishop's Lydeard (bus no. 218). Red sandstone cottages, church with carved bench-ends, inns. ½ mile from the bus stop at the Health Centre is the steam railway to Minehead.
Blagdon Hill (bus no. 208). Scenic ride. Alight at hilltop for view. Get on same bus as it returns to Taunton.
Bridgwater (buses no. 142, 143, 144, 246). Church, museum and Castle Street are worth visiting. A bore sweeps up the river when the tide turns.
Burrowbridge (bus no. 266 and short walk). Allermoor Pumping Station Museum.
+Crowcombe (bus no. 218). Winding valley road at foot of wooded hills. Thatched cottages, etc. Pretty footpath to Nether Stowey. Carew Arms for meals.
+East Combe (bus no. 218). On the scenic route to Minehead. Combe

Florey, a ¼-mile walk, is a very pretty red sandstone village with stream. Views of Quantock Hills.
+Hatch Court, Hatch Beauchamp (buses no. 495, or 496 and ¼ mile walk). Palladian mansion with fine furniture, china, Canadian militaria, deer park. Tea served.
Hornsbury Watermill (buses no. 494, 495, 496). Restaurant (and teas).
Hestercombe House, Kingston St Mary (bus no. 207). Lutyens gardens.
Ilminster (buses no. 494, 495, 496). See p. 153.
+Poundisford Park, Pitminster (bus no. 208: alight at Corfe turning). Tudor country house and garden, with fine views. Café.
Wellington (buses no. 202, 203). Fine landscape along this route. Wellington has an outstanding leisure centre and 16th-century church. Snuff cham-pionship in spring, flower show in sum-mer, carnival in autumn. Sheppy's Cider Museum and orchards are on this route.
Wiveliscombe (bus no. 205). Scenic ride, interesting church, inns. Views of Bren-don Hills.

Of the sights described the following are open nearly every day of the year: County Museum, Telecommunications Museum (Saturdays), Allermoor Pumping Station Museum.

SOME ANNUAL EVENTS July Festival (opera, mediaeval fair, etc.). **Aug.** Flower show in Vivary Park. **Sept.** River Struggle (Wellington to Taunton). **Oct.** Carnival (with barrel-rolling contest, illuminated procession, etc.). **Nov.** Music & Drama Festival.

TOURIST INFORMATION CENTRE Library, Corporation Street (0823 70479)
Publications obtainable from the Centre include: street plan (free); Dis-cover Taunton Deane, Taunton and en-virons – including folklore, etc. (30p);

Taunton mini-guide (10p), includes environs and maps; booklets of walks (50p) – this is good walking country; Somerset is the West Country (free) and other county publications; accommodation and restaurant guide (free); events lists (free).

ECONOMY TIPS Accommodation There are bargain breaks at the big hotels. Youth Hostel: Crowcombe. **Transport** For bargain tickets, see details on p. 143 (Sherborne). Taunton also has a Shop Farer ticket which allows unlimited travel for a week (outside peak periods) within the town. **Admissions** Of the places I've listed, the following are free: Sheppy's Cider Museum, Hestercombe gardens, Allermoor pumping station.

EARLY-CLOSING DAY Thursday.

MARKET DAYS General, Saturdays. Cattle, Tuesdays and Saturdays.

LOCAL ALE & FOOD Exmoor Ale. Cider. Clotted cream.

*This service was withdrawn during winter 1982–3 and at the time of going to press it was not known what service would operate during the summer.

TO WORCESTER
from Cheltenham

Coaches depart approximately every 2 hours and the journey takes about an hour. It skirts the fertile Vale of Evesham, with views of the Malvern Hills.

The coach started its journey through an area of market gardening and greenhouses in the foreground, with the jagged outline of the hills as a backdrop – blue and hazy in the heat of the day. Midsummer's presence was all around: in the bales of hay that dotted the fields, the poppies by the wayside and the briar roses or creamy elderflowers of the hedgerows. The few clouds in the brilliant blue sky, reflected in a bright blue river, looked as if they had been painted on with a palette knife. Fields of wheat were a bluish-green (all the yellows and light greens of spring fields were long gone).

Part of the motorway was under repair, so the coach slowed down to weave its way through lanes indicated by thousands of scarlet-and-white 'witches' hats' for a while, before picking up speed. We whisked by rows of poplars, straight as grenadiers; and by willows trailing their silvery-grey skirts into trickling streams. The shadow accompanying our coach was pencil-thin, with the midday sun almost directly overhead.

And so, downhill through leafy suburbs of Georgian and Victorian houses, we made the descent into Worcester – its great cathedral tower dominating the skyline. There were quick glimpses of tipsy black-and-white houses, the Commandery (described on p. 161), the red sandstone gateway to the cathedral precincts, old churches and the stone bridge with boys fishing and canoeing on the waters beyond.

The coach drew up in what is certainly one of the most attractive coach stations in England: right by lawns on the river bank. After a hot journey, what could be more refreshing than to sit here a while (with a cold drink from the café) to watch the boats go by? In fact, it is from this spot that boat trips start, an ideal way in which to view the town and its environs before exploring further on foot.

Cathedral City and Royalist Stronghold

From the coach station, a very pleasant way to approach the cathedral and all that surrounds it is by walking along the riverside, watching the boats and ducks go past. The path passes 'the glover's needle' and its terraced rose gardens (the needle is the slender spire, all that remains, of St Andrew's church); it goes past the *Severn Voyager* (you can have tea on board); and under rows of shady limes and beeches. If you were to continue far enough you would come to Diglis Canal Basin, lively with small craft.

I turned off, however, to visit the Royal Worcester porcelain factory where, apart from tours of the historic factory itself to see china being made and decorated, there is an excellent museum, with audiovisual show, as well as two shops – at one, 'seconds' attract bargain-hunters, particularly during the January and July sales. There is so much to see that the presence of a café is a welcome addition. Because the factory tours are very popular it is wise to book ahead (tel. 0905 23221).

Further on is the busy City Walls Road, along which the coach has entered. Among the antique shops in this area is The Commandery, one of Worcester's most ancient buildings (far larger than it seems from the road). Here Charles II had his headquarters during the Civil War and one room is filled with displays about the battle of Worcester, the Royalists' final defeat in 1649. Inside is a great hall with minstrels' gallery and hammerbeam roof, its bosses ornately carved. The house contains collections of armour, Jacobean furniture and reconstructions of old workshops (glovemaker, cobbler, cooper and blacksmith). Everywhere is the smell of beeswax polish. The Museum's range of booklets is particularly interesting, there are kits for children, a café, and a canalside garden with views of locks, narrow-boats and former glove factories. The Commandery deserves a visit of several hours.

The cathedral is only a few yards away. Through the great gateway of reddish-cream sandstone is quiet College Green, so-called because all the surrounding Georgian houses are now part of King's School. Worcester Cathedral has very lovely cloisters with windows looking onto grass, graves and white roses. The cathedral interior is richly decorated – rib-vaulting, angels, gilded bosses, colourful monuments of alabaster, a marble pulpit and a font with pinnacle cover rising roof-high. Its crypt and chapter house are both unique, and the great organ fills one of the transepts. This is the cathedral where King John chose to be buried, and from his tomb one gets the best view of the glorious east end. Prince Arthur (first husband of Catherine of Aragon) also lies here, in an elaborately decorated chantry chapel – too elaborate for Protestant tastes, which is why many figures of saints were deliberately defaced. (The cathedral has a café.)

Outside the west door are terraces and a walled garden where catmint and valerian thrive, leading to the yews and lawns of another Georgian green beyond which stands a new statue of Elgar (unveiled by the Prince of Wales in 1981) near what was once his father's music shop.

Across the road is Friar Street. I lingered among its antique and art shops; peered into the Tudor House museum of social history and the wine bars; and sat a while in the cobbled courtyard of Greyfriars which is overlooked by a gateway with scarlet-and-gold coats-of-arms and the message 'Except the Lord Build the House, Their Labour is but Lost that Build'. There is a carving of a Franciscan here, for once this was a pilgrims' hostel run by the monks. Sunlight and shade dappled this quiet corner, where Canterbury bells filled terracotta pots and roses scrambled up the old brick walls.

I turned down Pump Street to find the pedestrianised shopping centre of the town and the grandest of Guildhalls, built in 1721. It has not only both Charles I and Charles II in shining gold, robed and crowned, but Queen Anne too – not to mention a tremendous panoply of spears and halberds inside, along with portraits of civic worthies, and an assembly room resplendent with chandeliers. (The Tourist Information Centre is here.)

There is much more to Worcester than this, of course; but I had too little time to explore the City Museum of natural history (it has Saturday morning sessions for children), Art Gallery or Fort Royal Park (the battle site), for example. I was sorry not to have had longer in Worcester, a town that repays unhurried wandering down arcades or narrow lanes of mediaeval origin, and among ancient houses or inns.

SOME MORE PLACES TO VISIT For bus times and route map, tel. 0905 23296; also for booklet called A Day Out in the Country Without the Car. The region around Worcester is known as The Vales: a garden-like area, with varied hills, rivers and villages.

Avoncroft Museum (bus no. 144 and ¼ mile walk). Open-air museum of historic buildings, including a working windmill open to view. Demonstrations.

+Barbourne (buses no. W28, W31, W33, W38). Gheluvelt Park.

Bevere Island and lock (bus no. 303). Riverside walks.

+British Camp (bus no. X43 or X44 on Sundays). The most scenic views in the Malvern Hills, from Iron Age campsite, along Jubilee Drive. Hang-gliding. Kettle Sings café. Parks.

Bromsgrove (bus no. 144). Norton Museum of music boxes and Victoriana (with café). Parks.

+Bromyard (buses no. 419, 420). Market town with good walks in the surrounding downs. Lower Brockhampton house (National Trust) is a ½-mile walk from the bus stop.

Droitwich (bus no. 144). Now being revived as a spa with brine swimming pool. Black-and-white houses. Heritage Centre.

Evesham (buses no. 191, 251 – pretty routes – or X51, X52). Old market town with stocks on the green, Almonry Museum, inns, river boats, waterfront restaurant.

Hartlebury (bus no. 303). County museum (archaeology, crafts, etc). Castle.

Holt Fleet (bus no. X93 and ½-mile walk). Scenic route. River bridge built by Telford. Pub food at inn.

Inkberrow (buses no. 350, 351). Village of thatch and half-timbering (the Ambridge of 'The Archers'; one of the inns is the Archers' Bull Inn); at its best in blossom time.

Lower Broadheath (buses no. 310–12, 315, 316 and ½-mile walk). Elgar's birthplace. The cottage is now a museum.

+**Malvern Wells** (buses no. X41–X44). For footpaths up into the hills; spectacular views from these mini-mountains.

Ombersley: Clack's Farm (bus no. 303 and 1½-mile walk). The television garden: open second Sunday in every summer month.

Pershore (buses no. 191, 251, X51, X52). A main road through orchard and farm scenery, prettiest in spring. Abbey. Georgian houses.

Stourport (bus no. X93). Scenic route with pretty villages, to old riverside town. Canal basin. Lock, Stock and Barrel for lunches.

Teme Valley (buses no. 310, 312, 313, 417, 419, 420). Through hopfields to Clifton-on-Teme.

Upton-on-Severn (buses no. 372–5). Main road to riverside town, with half-timbered houses, waterfront inns and marina. Can take boat back to Worcester; or riverside path to Severn Stoke and then bus.

All the above can be visited nearly every day of the year, except for some that close in winter: Avoncroft, Norton Museum, Almonry Museum, County Museum.

SOME ANNUAL EVENTS April Blossom time. **May** Regattas. **July** Carnival. Civic Day. **Aug.** Three Choirs Festival (triennial: next at Worcester in 1984). **Sept.** Regatta. **Dec.** Christmas Oratorio and carols at cathedral. NB. There will be special events in 1984, the cathedral's novocentenary. The best months for picking your own fruit are May/June and Sept.

TOURIST INFORMATION CENTRE Guildhall (0905 23471)

Publications obtainable from the Centre include: Mini-guide, with town plan (10p); Official Guide – it covers environs too (50p); street plan (free);

Worcester: A Great Day Out (free); Tour of Worcester – illustrated historic trail (25p); A Walk Around the City (free); Byway Cycling in the West Midlands (£1.50); and free fact sheets on – where to stay, where to eat, pub grub, touring from Worcester (includes bus details), museums in Worcestershire, antique dealers, booksellers, history of The Guildhall, what's on (monthly); Charles II's escape route, Worcester to Shoreham in Sussex (25p).

The Centre has information about guided walks of the city; tours of cathedral, porcelain factory and local newspaper printing (the oldest newspaper in Britain); boat trips and boats for hire.

ECONOMY TIPS Accommodation Bargain breaks, and discounts for pensioners at the Gifford Hotel. **Transport** Severntickets entitle a passenger (or, at weekends, two adults and two children) to almost unlimited travel over a wide area around Worcester, for a month. Explorer tickets (see p. 206) can be used to go to Bridgnorth (Severn Valley Steam Railway), Ludlow (castle), Hereford (cathedral), Ledbury (see text), Gloucester (cathedral), Tewkesbury (abbey), Broadway (Cotswolds), Stratford-on-Avon, Birmingham, Stourbridge (glassworks) and Wolverhampton. **Admissions** Of the places I have mentioned, the following are free: Guildhall, City Museum, Art Gallery, Commandery (during winter), Tudor House Museum, Royal Worcester museum.

MARKET DAYS Covered markets daily in The Shambles; Fridays and Saturdays, in the Cornmarket car park; on Wednesday to Saturday in Blackfriars Market Hall. Cattle market, Mondays. Wholesale fruit and vegetable market, daily (with auctions on most days).

EARLY-CLOSING DAY Thursday.

LOCAL ALE & FOOD Farmhouse cheeses. Wye and Severn salmon and trout. Fruit. Asparagus. Worcestershire sauce. Dough-cakes. Tewkesbury mustard. Cider. Real ales – Banks's. Three Choirs and Bodenham wine.

A TOUR OF THE NORTH

My previous coach trips had been of only a few days each. Now I was off for much longer, to cover a 700-mile route with stops at five cities along the way. The distances of some journeys were greater than previously, yet even though I am a 6-footer with an arthriticky back, I did not find that hours in a coach were taxing.

The character of the places where I stayed was different from previous destinations: they were mainly industrial cities, some of them huge. For I had deliberately chosen, this time, to avoid such conventional magnets as York or Chester and to stay at places not ordinarily thought of as tourist centres. It seemed to me that no city which has its origins hundreds or even thousand of years ago could be lacking in character and interest, and so it proved. Further, each was totally different from the others.

Large cities can make a good change from seaside or country towns. In all weathers, they have certain things to offer which smaller places rarely provide in such abundance. For example, art galleries with exhibits of international fame. Theatres and concert halls that can afford top artistes and companies like the Royal Shakespeare or the Hallé Orchestra. Museums fit to compare with London's best (but not jammed with London's crowds), often free. Good public transport networks – also sometimes free. Plenty of restaurants, speciality shops and entertainments. Large swimming pools, leisure centres and – a uniquely English institution – the finest of parks. They often have rivers and canals with boat trips; and a good selection of bus or coach tours. There is usually plenty to do on Sundays, and after dark, and out of season.

And another thing. Many big cities have a modern university. And that means two things for the tourist: first, a campus likely to be open to visitors, providing a variety of amenities from parklands to avant-garde theatre, art exhibitions to sports centres; and secondly the possibility (outside term-time) of excellent, low-cost accommodation, either with meals or self-catering – for more about this, see p. 17.

And yet, even in cities that are huge by any standard except that of London, a bus may take one out to coast or countryside within about half-an-hour at most.

There was a heatwave when I went: was my tour really a good idea, I wondered? Perhaps the millions heading for resorts were right after all. But I found that, with the help of street maps (particulary city 'trails'), it is easy to walk where no fast traffic goes, and to relax in the quiet, green oases which usually only the locals know.

The interesting parts of a city are often close together in one compact area; and, these days, the pedestrianisation of many streets makes walking a pleasure. Cities that motorists regard as a nightmare (seen only from flyovers or not at all from underpasses) can look very different to a walker of byways and park footpaths. Traffic congestion and parking problems do not bother the rider on coach or bus.

As it turned out, no trip that I made in the course of writing this book proved more fascinating than this rather unusual one. It was more original, and hugely enjoyable. I returned home feeling fresh as a breeze.

TO SHEFFIELD

The service described here goes twice a day and the journey takes about 2½ hours. It goes through flat agricultural land to the coalfields of the Midlands. There are 9 other journeys taking 1¼ hours longer.

I had many times passed the Royal National Hotel in Bloomsbury (London's university quarter) without realising that its basement is used as a quite large coach station. It was from here, I learnt, that my journey north was to start.

I boarded the Rapide coach (run jointly by Wallace Arnold and National Express) in the early evening; only a few other people were on board. There were no queues or crowds around, by contrast with Victoria coach station which, staggering under the extra load imposed by the rail strike that summer, was daily providing television programmes with scenes of confusion as holidaymakers poured in by the thousand, suffering hours of delay. Rather smugly, I congratulated myself on having chosen to do the opposite of the majority. 'Going *north* for pleasure? And to an *industrial* city? To spend a *summer Sunday* there?' Friends were incredulous. But my policy was starting to pay off already, with a hassle-free start to the journey.

The coach was comparable with the Rapide to Plymouth (p. 111), and the journey was very smooth and fast.

We swung out into Tavistock Square, where Gandhi sits cross-legged incongruously in the middle of an exceedingly English flowerbed of pink geraniums, sharing the Square with somnolent figures sprawled in deckchairs and a bust of Louisa Aldrich-Blake (a pioneer of women's lib in medicine). We passed Lutyens' building for the British Medical Association; another of London's eccentricities, St Pancras church with pagan caryatids (the church is a copy of the temple of Erechteus); and the old stone lodges of Euston Station still incised with the names of exotic destinations like

St Petersburg which the steam trains used to serve. Then up Albany Street – which has a curiously named pub, The Queen's Head and Artichoke – and into Prince Albert Road where stately mansions overlook the colourful craft in the Regent's Canal basin, Primrose Hill (no primroses – but druids gather at the solstices, and the story persists that Queen Boadicea was buried here), Lord Snowdon's huge aviary in the Zoo, and Regent's Park itself. Avenue Road, flanked by the homes of tycoons and diplomats, leads to Swiss Cottage and beyond that lies the M1.

The first part of this is the route that I described on pp. 103–4; but months had passed since I last travelled it; and now the wheatfields were the colour of cornflakes, the hedges were high and blowsy, and the verges brilliant with rose bay willow herb, sometimes aptly called fireweed. There were sun-umbrellas outside inns, golfers trod the greens, and magpies swooped across the fields. But this cannot be called a really attractive route. The country is too flat and the road monotonously straight. Pylons stride across the landscape, and every so often factories or some distant city loom above the fields, or else a cluster of cooling towers, steaming away in unison like a coven of witches' cauldrons.

We were about half way when we entered Leicestershire, county of cheese and steeplechasing – and there, sure enough, were the herds of cows and the lush green grass needed for the former and the needle-sharp spires of the churches for the latter.

We crossed the River Trent, with pleasure-boats moored near a frothing weir (this is the boundary of Nottinghamshire) and passed a huge reservoir, its surface set ablaze by the low rays of the brassy evening sun. Derbyshire followed, with the dominating profile of Hardwick Hall (built by Bess of Hardwick, of whom more later) up on a small hill. From here on, with changing geology, farms were more often of stone than of brick. Collieries and coal-tips multiplied.

The sky was no longer all-blue. Sombre clouds had gathered, but were dramatically illuminated beneath by streaks of incandescent orange, the sun's last fling before nightfall.

Ahead, the whole landscape gradually filled with the huge sprawl of Sheffield. We threaded our way in past some of the cutlery and tool factories on which the city's greatness was built, past colourful canal-boats and soot-blackened stone walls (a reminder of what the entire city looked like before the great clean-up of the 1960s), and came to a halt in the huge, untidy coach station: one of the four biggest interchange points in Britain.

City of Steel

After a rather long and hot journey, I was glad of a shower, followed by a comfortable bed. This faced a big window (which I flung wide to let in the evening breeze and the last sleepy chirp of birds) with a view across trees to hills on which the lights of distant houses sparkled through the twilight. I had ample pillows, quiet and good lighting for a read: three things often lacking in even expensive hotels. Yet this was not even a hotel (see p. 205).

The next morning was a Sunday: ideal for some gentle sightseeing after a 4-course breakfast, as the noisy hustle of weekdays was stilled and one could walk and look about in peace. Plenty of Sheffield's 'sights' open their doors on Sundays, and my only problem was which to go and see. Like many cities, Sheffield has more of interest than some conventional tourist resorts.

Close by the central bus and coach station is a towpath from which to watch the canal-boats but, better still, on Sundays the *May Queen* takes passengers on canal trips. I found her waiting by the bank of a small garden tucked away at the end of a former wharf. The old warehouses, with gaping panes, are slowly being restored. On the cobbles, a family of ducks waddled among families working on the maintenance of the many small craft that are based here. The *May Queen* follows the canal from Canal Basin, passing alongside steel foundries, tool manufacturers, stock yards and other industrial sites synonymous with Sheffield's industrial heritage. The journey ends, after a six-mile trip, at the impressive flight of eleven locks at Tinsley. Before long the canal may be busy again, with the help of an EEC grant – not just with the local barges (known as 'tom puddings') but with 700-tonne giants carrying coal and aggregates to the east coast, for export.

Within a few minutes by bus is Sheffield's latest pride, its Industrial Museum – formerly the generating station for electric trams. The old buildings are on a city-centre island in the middle of the dark waters of the River Don (not as polluted as it looks for there are reeds, ferns, rushes, and marsh flowers as well as ducks paddling under the sooty walls). The whole place has an impressive personality. Looming high above the granite setts, iron bollards and former gas-lamps is a colossal Dalek-like structure: one of the last Bessemer converters used for smelting steel. A kind of pressure-cooker, it stood over a furnace which was never allowed to go out for half a century. Cold and still the convertor now stands, while spiders spin their shining threads across its black angles. As to the museum itself, Sheffield would be worth a visit for this alone. Beautifully laid out, it is a temple to the great days of steel-making.

I began by studying the animated visual that explains how each different kind of steel is made. All round me were the clicks and whines of exhibits in motion – massive pieces of engineering, or tiny models. The canal's history from 1819 was graphically told, too. But Sheffield's connection with steel, coal and waterways goes back much further than this: in 1630, 28 cutlers already had their wheels grinding away, driven by the many streams that run down the valleys and into the Don: it was the availability of this waterpower that started the great cutlery industry going. By 1740, with more sophisticated techniques in use, Sheffield was making half of Europe's cutlery.

Silversmithing followed, and beautiful craft-made exhibits are on show. But – past the moving steam-hammer with simulated red-hot ingots, past the intact workshop of a penknife-maker (in use until 20 years ago), past a tiny peepshow of a hand-rolling mill in action, past such fanciful exhibits as Victorian ice-skates shaped like a heron – past all these, I found the most absorbing show of all: a 'street' of Little Mesters' workshops. The Little Mesters were the one-man businesses which used to be so typical of Sheffield, each man with his own craft specialism. And here some of them still are: one man forging, the next grinding and a third finishing. I talked with the old grinder as he worked on blades for farriery knives ordered by the Canadian Royal Mounties. One in four is left-handed, he told me – and that it was here that the original Bowie knife was made (for Colonel Bowie of Alamo fame). His next job would be chiropodists' scalpels. This is, in every sense, a 'working' museum. Its most spectacular working exhibit is a colossal engine of 12,000 h.p. which powered a rolling-mill for armourplate up to 1955 and then another for the heavy plate required in nuclear reactors and oil rigs, up to 1978.

A short bus ride away, beyond the many acres of wooded hills near Beauchief Abbey, is Abbeydale – an industrial hamlet that, from hundreds long vanished, has been preserved for visitors to see. Here the smells of iron, wood and coal still linger, and the splashing sound of water led me to a large old workshop where great waterwheels still power huge grindstones and much else. Massive timbers groan, pistons swish gently up and down. They power a Heath Robinson – but entirely practical – network of implements, from metal-cutters to the bellows at the forge. There is a further series of small workshops, each with its own forge and anvil. The first lead smelters settled here in Norman times. Beyond rooms used as a museum, the Dickensian clerks' office has been preserved too:

high stools, guttered candles, leather ledgers with copper-plate handwriting.

Although it is this industrial history that makes Sheffield uniquely interesting it has a lively cultural side too – and superb scenery up in its enclosing hills (and beyond them, for the Peak District is only a bus-ride away). For example, within a few minutes' walk of the central bus and coach station are the Perpendicular cathedral and the Graves gallery (with a notable collection of European and oriental art). Just behind the cathedral is Paradise Square, an unspoilt Georgian square, where Wesley often preached.

Short bus-rides away, I found the particularly lovely Botanical Gardens on a hillside, with 18 acres of flowers, lawns and an elegant early Victorian conservatory; and, in the university quarter further north, another art collection, the Mappin Gallery (this one concentrates on 18th- to 20th-century British paintings: Turner, Constable, the pre-Raphaelites) and also the City Museum (which has good exhibits on local natural history, as well as a collection of Sheffield cutlery and plate).

Sheffield is a good city for bus-riding and, in the centre, buses are free. Although some stretches of road are ugly, there is more than compensation in the spectacular views that regularly pop into sight, for high hills form a ring around the centre. Sheffield has a great many parks and woods up on those hillsides, too: they are not all workers' stone cottages, chapels and breweries of Victorian vintage, nor the high-rise blocks of our own time. (In fact, there is a circular walk of 10 miles which goes through park after park.)

I had time for only one other facet of Sheffield: the Mary Queen of Scots connection. To the south-east, on yet another of those hills, stands a lonely Tudor turret with a few ruined fortifications in the surrounding grass. Its windows are lozenge-paned, and on the roof above is a small cupola. Butterflies fluttered among the lavender bushes near the door, and all around (where once there was a deer park) stood a modern housing estate. This is Sheffield Manor where Mary was held prisoner for about a third of her life, in the charge of the Earl of Shrewsbury and his wife, the redoubtable

Bess of Hardwick. Was Mary consoled by the views from here, the fine plaster ceilings and heraldic fireplaces in this turret built specially for her? The windy site did not suit her: she suffered from rheumatism. Her story is told in a book by Keith Cheetham on sale at the Tourist Information Centre.

MORE PLACES TO VISIT (by bus) include: **Bishop's House** mediaeval yeoman's house and social history museum. **Graves Park** 200 acres, with nature trail. **Ladies Spring Wood** a nature reserve of special scientific interest. **Rivelin Dam and Rocks** a nature trail goes through superb scenery, punctuated with old grinding-wheels along the river. **Whinfell** quarry gardens. **Whirlow Brook Park** secluded rock and water gardens, and exotic flowers. **Whiteley Woods** with the Shepherd Wheel – a water-powered grindery that still works. **Wortley Top Forge** water-driven, 17th century.

For a bus and rail route map of the area, bus times, bus tours, etc., tel. 0742 28631. For other information, booklets, street plans, events, etc., tel. the Tourist Information Centre, 0742 734760.

TO NEWCASTLE

Coaches depart from Sheffield about 5 times a day and the journey takes about 4½ hours (including a ¾-hour break at Leeds). It goes through some tremendous scenery in north Yorkshire. Interesting stops along the way include Ripon (with its abbey) and Durham (castle and cathedral).

After the coach had gone a mile or two, I glanced back for a clear view of Sheffield sheltering within its ring of hills. We wound our way at first through a largely industrial landscape; whenever a stretch of woodland survived, it soon gave way to dark satanic chimneys again, or coal-tips. But this did not last for long: one of the best stretches of the M1 followed, among rolling hills, woodlands, footpaths through bracken, and field after field of grain that was now brown as toast. We passed what must have been a deer farm, with dozens of young ones grazing in a paddock.

For once, I did not mind when occasionally cuttings through the hills cut us off from the superb views, for at this time of year the high embankments are crammed with wildflowers and as colourful as any herbaceous border: pink fireweed, in particular, and great drifts of yellow ragwort – but dozens of others too (purple thistles, huge daisies, sorrel, vetch, scabious and many more).

We turned into Leeds, passing gasometers, featureless modern blocks and a canal with water splashing down its lock-gates. I had to change coaches here, with a half-hour wait in a small and sleazy coach station which has no attractions except for a graffiti-collector ('Humpty Dumpty was pushed' said one. Below another, too scatalogical to print here, was the comment 'Nice writing. A shame about the brain.'). But at the back of the coach station I discovered a pleasant retreat, York Place, where the sedate Georgian houses have basements now used for wine bars and bistros.

The outward route showed Leeds to better advantage, with a view along the main street (The Headrow) flanked by handsome civic buildings, followed by a green with Georgian houses, and then

J.A.MAROT

cricketers playing on a hilltop near the stump of an old windmill – but the inevitable high-rise blocks dominated. Soon, however, we were among a patchwork of fields, woods, hills and valleys again, and then running alongside the walls surrounding Harewood House with a great gateway like a triumphal arch. The sunshine filtered through the trees as the road pursued its serpentine course, often with far views. We crossed the River Wharfe (shallow, wide and winding, with an ancient stone bridge), passing haymakers at work and neatly clipped sheep with black faces. A huge viaduct of thirty arches strode across a wide valley.

Then there came walls of millstone grit or else high hedges concealing prosperous suburban houses built from honey-coloured stone: the outskirts of Harrogate. We moved past crescents and greens, avenues of chestnuts, a roundabout of massed antir-

rhinums, brilliantly pink or yellow. Lacey ironwork, hanging-
baskets, lawns, formal flowerbeds, wide parades and canopied
shops led towards the spa's historic heart, the old Pump Rooms.

Out again we went, among the grand hotels (even guesthouses
are grand in Harrogate), to regain the rural scene once more, where
streams and cows filled the foreground and a lush landscape spread
out to the far horizon. We kept crossing streams and rivers – from
one bridge (modern), we could see another (old) where children sat
swinging their legs. There were many such hump-backed stone
bridges, many leisurely games of cricket, secluded mansions, old
milestones and huge square-towered churches adding variety to a
landscape which was one of the most spectacular in this book.

Then Ripon's abbey appeared on the skyline and soon we
were crossing the calm, wide river and threading our way among
half-timbered and bay-windowed houses to the big market square
with the ancient Wakeman's House. Unfortunately, the coach
paused too briefly in Ripon (where a wakeman still sounds his horn
at the curfew hour) for me to follow the path which leads from the
coach park to the abbey. (Ripon is described in my *England by Bus*.)

The fields became bigger and bigger, vast hedgeless expanses
of wheat or glossy-leaved beet. A helicopter flew low, spraying
crops. Back on the fast A1, we joined a stream of traffic through a
flat and monotonous landscape under a pallid sky. We crossed the
River Tees and thus entered County Durham. Fine parks and
houses of dignity stand on this side of Darlington, and we had a
superb view of the church (its tall spire is exceptional) beyond the
willow-fringed river which is crossed by a pretty, balustraded
bridge: not the industrial aspect usually associated with this town.
The next stretch of the A1 was more interesting – cows dozed among
buttercups with the outline of the Pennine Hills beyond, blue and as
if veiled in gauze.

The huge, resolute tower ahead of us could be only one thing:
Durham's Norman cathedral. We had a good view downhill as we
entered the city: of the river that curves nearly all round the rock
which cathedral and castle share, and a sharawaggi of rooftops. But
in a minute the perspective was reversed, with the cathedral tower-

ing above us and the red brick houses, too, piled up on the steep slopes. From the bridge, there was a glimpse of the frothing weir.

Back, then, to the main road, passing the castellated turrets of Lumley Castle (now a hotel, which runs Elizabethan banquets – a very popular entertainment throughout the north-east) before arriving at the smoking factory chimneys of Gateshead on the outskirts of Newcastle. The coach moved fast, leaving me with a medley of impressions (the several bridges over the Tyne, water-front cranes downstream, the cathedral's exquisite 'lantern' tower, church ruins, the classical façades for which Newcastle is famous) before it came to a halt in the Gallowgate coach station.

Monks and the Maritime Connection

Newcastle upon Tyne is a city of considerable architectural splendour; and with a history that starts long before the Romans set up camp here.

I had stayed overnight near its adjacent town, Gateshead, enjoying the leafy breezes from Saltwell Park – the finest park in the north; with woods, rose gardens, lake and aviary – and then visiting the excellent Shipley Art Gallery next morning. Not long ago, a vast Tintoretto was discovered mouldering in a vault of Newcastle Cathedral. Now restored, it hangs among other comparable art treasures here. The gallery houses a crafts centre too, and when I was there patchwork (a speciality of the north-east) was being demonstrated, with historic quilts hung on the walls. For visitors with more vigorous interests, there is a good leisure centre, too, at Gateshead.

Once back in Newcastle, I found that the city's walking-tour leaflet was ideal for my purposes, since the recommended trail starts near the coach station and goes downhill to the waterfront via Blackfriars. This former Dominican monastery for preaching friars now houses not only the Tourist Information Centre, craft workshops, an excellent café, a lawn with seats and an exhibition about the Dominicans but also a first-rate museum explaining Newcastle's origins, which doubled the interest of what I was about to see in the streets beyond.

After Henry VIII's dissolution of the monasteries, the buildings were used as meeting places for the city's trade guilds, and some of the rooms are still furnished accordingly. In one, I sat with other viewers around an oval table, pressed a button, and a vivid re-enactment took place of more than a million years of change on this site. The 'magic' map in front of us showed ice ages come and go, early settlements spring up, Roman roads, the building of the 'new castle' by the Normans, then the city walls, and the steady spread of industry and homes. The show over, I went to the next room which has a dozen miniature cross-sections of some notable Newcastle buildings – each from a different architectural period, and with actual samples of the materials used at that period. In a third room, an audiovisual show described the industries of Newcastle – but with no smooth-voiced commentator. Instead, the workers' own voices recalled everyday life in the shipyards, factories, breweries and railways.

In Blackfriars you can buy anything from leather clogs to a patchwork cot-quilt or a record of Geordie (that is, Newcastle) songs which are still sung in that great Northumbrian institution, the working men's clubs. Or you can watch archaeologists excavating the monastery church. Blackfriars is half a day's entertainment in itself.

Streets wind steeply down from here, past remnants of the city walls, to Dean Street (where bistros, antique dealers and craft shops congregate) and a cobbled byway between the mediaeval cathedral (floodlit at night) and the Norman castle. The gatehouse of the latter houses a bagpipe museum: Northumbrian pipes differ from the Scottish variety, making a more civilised sound, Geordies claim – you can hear them played at the museum and judge for yourself.

Further still lies the historic waterfront, with Guildhall (it houses a 'flea market' on Saturdays), quays (Sunday markets), the mediaeval Cooperage, the Baltic Tavern for seafood meals (at a price), Trinity House (a museum of lighthouse and maritime safety history), a fine Custom House and views of Newcastle's many and varied bridges. Beyond Trinity House is a quiet corner for a pause or picnic, with grass between old walls. Footpaths and steps lead one upwards again, dodging the flyovers and fast one-ways that make Newcastle a nightmare for motorists, and with intriguing views at each turn.

Much of Newcastle's finest architecture is attributable to John Dobson who, in the 1820s, designed one noble building after another. Many still remain, giving the city its unique character: Grey Street, with monument at the top, is world-famous. The wide, formal roads are designed for vistas, and the classical late-Georgian buildings harmonise with one another. Despite some ruthless chopping up in our own time, Newcastle still has a handsome wholeness, best appreciated with feet on the ground rather than on accelerator and brake, and often unexpected views of it spring into sight when walking the alleys and passageways.

A little breathless, one arrives at the 17th-century almshouses now known as the Joicey Museum: a quiet retreat even though the traffic swirls around on flyways at roof-level. Each little bedroom is now a mini-museum with its own theme: one, for instance, houses Bewick's wood engravings and a reconstruction of his workbench; in another there is a diorama of old Newcastle and, at the press of a button, the great flood of 1771 is re-enacted (it swept away the original bridge, which had houses on it, like old London Bridge) and the catastrophic fire of 1854 – complete with the sound of crackling wood and screaming victims. Shooting game on the moors is very popular with the workers of Newcastle, so a tower room houses a celebrated collection of locally made guns (with audiovisual); and the armourer's workshop from Alnwick Castle is now here, complete down to the last rivet and even the furnace ash. In a series of furnished rooms (Stuart to the present day) children are encouraged to try on Cromwellian armour or use the 1900 telephone. Every mid-December, there is a queue to sample soup made from the recipe of a Victorian soup kitchen for the poor, while in summer there are brass-rubbing and war-gaming sessions. A small courtyard provides an opportunity to rest or picnic.

Great though Newcastle is, its green belt is quickly reached by bus (there can be few cities of this size where cows graze only ½ mile from the Civic Centre). Leazes Park is a vast area by the university (with flowers, tennis and a boating lake) but much more picturesque is Jesmond Dene in a valley with rocks and waterfall, near which many of the smaller hotels and the youth hostel are found. Artists hang out their work here on Sundays, and there is another seafood restaurant.

There was much more to see in the city, had I been able to stay longer. Right in the centre is a vast and very modern shopping centre, wrapped round Georgian Eldon Square (it even includes a Victorian market with Marks & Spencer's first 'penny bazaar'). I preferred the characterful old Handyside Arcade opposite this Centre. (Most of the city buses go out from the bus station in the Centre: the three other bus stations serve the environs to north, west and south. The Centre also incorporates a super Leisure Centre with all the usual indoor sports.) Only a matter of yards away is the Laing Art Gallery which houses British art of international importance – from the 18th century to today.

There are two more outstanding museums within a short bus-ride, or even walk: the Hancock, for natural history, and the Museum of Science and Engineering – second only to London's Science Museum. But one could go on and on – photographic museum, the *Turbinia* (the world's first turbine-driven ship), arts workshop, theatres, the gardens and statuary of the modern Civic Centre: like much else, these are all quickly accessible on foot, by bus or using the city's smart new underground railway (Metro) which even goes as far afield as the coast: a fascinating coast, incidentally, which I have described in my book *England by the Sea*.

The Metro will, by 1984, provide one way to reach Jarrow (as an alternative to the buses) where the remains of Bede's monastery overlook the Tyne and its shipping. Like other museums in the county of Tyne & Wear, the Bede museum is exceptional. I started by learning the story of the monastery from an audiovisual with actors playing monks. Bede's monastery became a centre for producing the richest of illuminated manuscripts, now in museums worldwide, and the earliest stained glass. Excavated fragments of the monks' tools and few possessions, displayed in the museum, are more meaningful after seeing the pictures of these in use, and the tiny models of the monastery as it used to be. As I wandered round, the air filled with a recording of monks chanting (one of the exhibits is a letter from Bede recruiting a harpist). The ending of monastic life here was described in the Anglo-Saxon Chronicle, which speaks of flashes of light and fiery dragons in the sky presaging rapine, slaughter and 'the harrying of the heathen': in other words, Viking invasions.

In the café, one can eat Saxon-style bread and soups (using horn spoons); the excellent souvenir shop has Saxon replicas; and medicinal herbs of Bede's time are grown in the garden: penny-royal, comfrey, feverfew, tansy and rue. Incidentally, this is the only museum I know which has a pretty sitting-room with sofas for weary visitors, alongside a room for modern art or crafts shows. Outside are remains of the monastery and its church into which are built chunks from a Roman temple, proving how ancient a holy site this is.

MORE PLACES TO VISIT (by bus, or Metro) include: **Benwell** Roman temple. **Brunswick** nature reserve. **Burnopfield and Consett** route with spectacular views of countryside. **Derwent Valley** scenic walk in country park, from Rowlands Gill, with Gibside Chapel – Palladian. **Springwell** for Bowes rope-hauled and steam railway. **South Shields** great Roman fort; museum. **Sunderland** this town has Monkwearmouth Station Museum, art gallery with museum, aircraft museum, Grindon Museum of social life and St Peter's church with chapter-house. **Sulgrave** Washington F. Pit mining museum. **Sunniside** Tanfield steam railway and picturesque Causey Arch. **Thornley Wood** nature reserve. **Tynemouth** priory ruins, watchtower museum of the life brigade. **Washington** waterfowl park. **Washington Old Hall** home of George Washington's family. **Wylam** George Stephenson's cottage. **Whitley Bay** and **Cullercoats** seaside resorts.

For bus times, times of bus tours or Tyne & Wear County Transport Guide with map, tel. 0632 325325. For other information, booklets, street plans, guided walks, events, etc. tel. the Tourist Information Centre, 0632 615637 or 0632 610691.

TO CARLISLE

Coaches from Newcastle depart once or twice a day and the journey takes about 1½ hours. It goes through the lovely Tyne valley with views of the border hills to the north and the Pennine moors to the south. A good stop on the way is Hexham (for its magnificent abbey, and as a point from which to visit the Roman wall or Kielder's great man-made lake and forest).

The elderly coach belonged to a Scottish bus company (its ultimate destination was Glasgow), and there were plenty of Scottish voices on board as we shook and rattled our way out by terraces of Victorian working cottages. The far Pennine hills could be glimpsed hazily between them.

For most of the route, we were running through 'the debatable lands' over which Scots and English had fought for centuries. The Roman wall, built to keep the Scots out, lay a few miles out of sight to the north of the route (except at one point, on Newcastle's outskirts, where vestiges of it can be seen in the grass verge).

The road ran straight at first, between meadows where hay was lying to dry in the scorching heat or where it still grew high, with wildflowers among it. Some huge fields were full of ripe barley, in others sheep or highland cattle grazed. By the roadside, thistles and big harebells (the 'blue bells of Scotland') were another reminder that the border was not far off.

Sometimes there were deep tree-filled clefts where a stream ran down to join the River Tyne, or the underlying rock bared itself through the grass – the stone from which the local farms, the drystone walls and Hadrian's mighty wall itself were built.

Soon the grandeur of the scenery to come was already evident on the horizon. Some of the buildings in the pleasant old town of Corbridge are made from Roman stones: the great Roman fort nearby is well worth a visit.

We resumed the main road and, passing castellated Beaufront

Castle up on its hillside, were soon at Hexham. Its largely Norman abbey is bigger than many cathedrals, dominating the attractive market square.

After that, we saw rather more of the River Tyne (with which the road runs roughly parallel), following it so closely that every shining boulder in its shallow bed could be seen. Larch and ash cast long shadows in the late sun, still strong enough to make colours blaze – the scarlet of the poppies, the pink of rose bay willow herb.

In autumn, the hillsides are covered with purple heather; but even now they were colourful – a patchwork of greens and browns spreading down into the valleys between. There were occasional dark plantations of conifers, with birch trees providing a light touch at their edges.

The scenery became increasingly varied and beautiful as the road wound up and down. A weir, old bridge, and little houses by the waterside comprised the village of Haydon Bridge. Very typical

of the area, the stone cottages (with stone or slate roofs) had white sash windows and a multitude of bright flowers outside.

As the miles passed, the geology changed: boulders in the river bed were mainly reddish now. At Bardon Mill a big circular kiln is still in use, no longer for firing chimneys but to make big strawberry-pots, sold in local shops.

Occasionally, one spots a fortified farm with squat and castellated pele tower: another relic of border warfare (the cattle would be herded in below, the villagers would defend from above).

Up and down the road continued, vetch and clover by the wayside, pale-coated Charolais cattle grazing in the rich pastures between the copses, up on the hilltops bare moorland, and in the valleys trees and bracken.

Beyond Haltwhistle, where roses clambered on terraces of stone cottages, the road continued among fields that rose and fell, outstretched to the Scottish horizon. The verges were full of yarrow, lady's bedstraw and meadowsweet; green bracken grew high in the beech woods; and ferns sprouted from crevices in the drystone walls or the walls of great barns. It was evidently a good year for hay – barns were crammed with it, with haystacks alongside, and repeatedly we encountered tractor-drawn loads being borne along. The whole scene was one of abundance – even the cottage window-boxes could hardly be seen for the profusion of petunias and lobelia brimming over them. The barley fields were golden, the sheep (black-faced and curly-horned) looked plump. We passed a trout farm where bare-chested young men were busy with nets at the tanks.

At Brampton, the colour of the building stone began to change to a deep red. Brampton is an attractive place, with a green, cobbles in front of its moot hall and inns, and pleasantly varied houses around them – roofs varying in pitch, stucco in different colours. There was a short pause here before we continued by more sunlight-dappled streams and verges with grasses so long that their heads bowed under the weight of ripening seeds. To the right of the road stood an old abbey by the river. But soon the road straightened out, hurled itself across the busy M6 and past a cattle market, and brought us into the suburbs of Carlisle. There were glimpses of Victorian Carlisle: terraces behind neat rows of lime trees, red sandstone churches, the classical lettering of street names carved into stonework, and – very typical of Carlisle – decorative brick-work (the arrangement of bricks known as Flemish bond creates a chequered effect). We turned right at the Citadel, rebuilt about 1810 to house law courts and council offices; had a view of Lowther Street's dignified banks and wrought iron; and came to a halt in the coach station.

Two Thousand Years of Border History

The heart of old Carlisle is only a few steps from the coach station: the Market Square, which is the starting point of the walk recommended in Carlisle's 'town trail' leaflet. I found it an excellent route, and a quiet one too.

In the centre of the Square is a colourful 17th-century market cross, from the steps of which Bonnie Prince Charlie – on the first stage of his abortive march south from Scotland in 1745 – proclaimed his father King. The lion on top guards the book of city bye-laws in its paws. Behind stands the elegant pink town hall, early Georgian, with a double staircase leading up to the Tourist Information Centre; and further back is the much older Guildhall with grotesque figures carved among the mediaeval half-timbering (there is a local history museum inside).

I turned down tiny St Cuthbert's Lane, which has small shops, to find myself in a quiet green with beech trees and a Georgian church on one side: it has a blue-and-white gallery inside, and a movable pulpit on a kind of railway. I walked past the immense tithe barn (its ancient roof timbers visible through windows that have been put in) to emerge on top of the Norman city walls. Here the walk looks down over roofs and treetops to one side (with a huge, early cotton-mill in the distance), and has good views of the cathedral above red sandstone walls on the other. The houses along here include the deanery, which incorporates a Norman pele tower – one of the fortified houses which were so necessary in the centuries when wars between Scots and English were endemic.

An alley led me to Abbey Street, largely Georgian, and 17th-century Tullie House, surrounded by a garden where ancient stones and a Roman shrine catapult (replica) stand among the potentillas and wallflowers. Inside is a museum – very static and old-fashioned compared with those I had visited in Sheffield and Newcastle. Its Roman exhibits are the most interesting; sculpted tombstones of forgotten matrons and monuments to goddesses (a few Celtic gods too).

On the other side of Tullie House is Castle Street which leads down to the dramatically sited and very red Norman castle which withstood centuries of sieges and assaults – an exhibition tells its history. This was the first of many prisons for Mary Queen of Scots, though not in the gloomy dungeons where the sad graffiti of lesser prisoners can still be read. There are superb views from the ramparts and beyond lies parkland with riverside walks.

After retracing my footsteps, I turned into the cool shades of Long Lane (which has an interesting craft shop) as a short cut to Fisher Street. This is the place for browsing among antique, craft and bookshops, or others selling pikelets (scones) and pies, in Georgian or Victorian premises. The Dundas coffee bar combines snacks with a multiplicity of stalls selling anything from old postcards and books to Victorian babywear and pans; and twice a week, the local Women's Institutes bring in their produce for sale nearby. There's an excellent covered market, too, with ham cured in Cumberland-style, northern or Scottish specialities like black pudding and haggis, Cumberland rum butter and pats of butter impressed with cows' heads. Bargains, too, in earthenware or cheapjack fabrics – and two stalls for gourmets, one with nothing but cheeses, the other with every kind of coffee. The market is worth seeing for its architectural details as well.

Finally, Carlisle's greatest jewel – the mediaeval cathedral. After the heat of the day, I was glad to sit in the cool silence of the choir, the dark oak of the elaborately carved stalls contrasting with the brilliant colours elsewhere. The east window, in Decorated style, is enormous and dazzling, one of the finest in Europe; the coffered ceiling is blue with gold stars; great, coloured angels bear coats-of-arms aloft; and the cathedral was full of flowers that day. There is plenty of detail over which to linger – from the fossils in the pale stone slabs of the floor to the recently restored series of big paintings found on wood screens (15th-century picture-strips telling the stories of saints and apostles; now once more their colours are vivid). In a side chapel, the cathedral has a tremendous 16th-century Flemish altarpiece brought here, after restoration by the Victoria & Albert Museum, from a chapel near Penrith.

The cathedral needs an unhurried visit. There is the prior's room to see, too, in the pele tower (its ceiling timbers painted in the manner of some Scottish and Scandinavian mansions') and, a welcome end, a café in the undercroft of what was once the monks' refectory.

MORE PLACES TO VISIT (by bus) include: **Bowness** on the Solway Firth. Fine views of Scotland. Edward I monument is a mile walk across marshes. An area of outstanding natural beauty. **Brampton** see p. 184; market on Wednesdays. **Dalston** pretty village; for riverside walks, obtain guidebook from Carlisle's Tourist Information Centre. **Eden valley** lovely riverside drives, through woodlands and villages; at Armathwaite there are rapids. **Gilsland** Roman wall fort is 1¾-mile walk.

Gretna Green (in Scotland) old smithy and marriage rooms for elopers. **Penrith** a rose-red castle, quaint byways. **Talkin Tarn** lake with country park. **Wetheral** riverside walks to priory ruins; Corby Castle. **Wigton** market town – a pleasant ride towards Lake District scenery.

For information about bus times, day-return and Explorer tickets, tel. 0228 21038. For other information, booklets, street maps, events, tel. the Tourist Information Centre, 0228 25517.

TO LANCASTER

Coaches depart twice a day from Keswick, and the journey
takes about 2 hours. It goes through lakeland scenery with
waters reflecting the mountains above. A good stop on the way
would be Grasmere or Ambleside.

Carlisle is an excellent base from which to visit several of England's
best touring regions – the Scottish borders, the Eden valley, the
northern Pennines and, of course, the Lake District which was
where I wanted to visit friends (by bus) before resuming my tour.
(Because it was high summer, I found the lakeland towns and many
roads seething with tourists: Carlisle's byways had been tranquil by
comparison.) I returned to my coach tour at Keswick.

The coach left the town past houses built from slate blocks,
overtook bronze-backed walkers, and climbed high. Dry-stone
walls zigzagged up the sides of shapely hills where hay was waiting in
bales or bracken spread a green cloak. People were lunching at
wooden trestle tables outside low, whitewashed inns with roses
round their doors, while cattle slept in the noonday sunshine. We
climbed higher still, among thickets of birch or larch and rocks
jutting through greensward, with views of the long rippling lake
(Derwentwater). There were wayside chapels, old slate tombstones
and telephone boxes painted grey because the customary red would
strike a discordant note. Streams dashed down headlong through
grooves which it had taken millennia to carve in the hard volcanic
rock – contrasting with, a few minutes further, soft green sheep
pastures that were as billowy as an eiderdown.

The pass descended then, to a wide green valley with farms
sheltering in knots of trees. There were more slate-block houses at
Grasmere (a flowery, neat place with the Wordsworth museum at
Dove Cottage), a hump-backed bridge, children clambering on
rocky outcrops and a pause at a slate shelter for coach or bus
passengers (the starting point for guided walks up the fells). We
squeezed between craft shops, Sarah Nelson's 'original ginger-

bread' bakery, and cottages that are now guest-houses. Beyond, the waters of the mere sparkled and shone bright blue.

The coach passed from sunshine to shade in glens where bracken and last year's rusty leaves patterned the ground beneath the trees. Another blue lake (Rydal Water) came into view, reed-fringed, with the hills on the far side descending to the edge, clad with green bracken. I saw waterlilies, a stream, cheerful red-and-white sun umbrellas outside an inn and then Rydal Hall up on the hillside. More streams – picnickers – cows – sun, shade, and sun again: the summery scenes flashed by.

Ambleside, another busy little town, has the Lake District Historical Centre, and Victorian hotels where visitors still take tea at white cast-iron tables in grounds that overlook the lake (Windermere): this one dotted with white sails, small motor-boats, a pleasure launch and bathers around its shores.

Windermere town next, via meadows of wildflowers: its streets flanked by grey stone houses with decorative fretwork at their gables. Beyond we followed roads with burdock and vetch by the wayside and geese in a field, up to great heights from which to look across a multitude of small fields and copses in the wide valley to the hills beyond. The coach gave me a fine view over the tops of walls, to huge barns or into gardens abundant with flowers.

The descent into Kendal was steep. Here the rough-textured building-stone changed to the palest of greys. In Kendal's shady bus station, there was a reshuffle of passengers. The coach that had started half empty was now more than full and, a second one being on its way to relieve the pressure, people bound for London were put onto the latter for a fast journey all the way. The rest of us spread ourselves out once again.

The journey improved all the time. We went over an old stone bridge that crosses the wide and shallow river where ducklings and terns floated and children paddled, then passed a church beautifully sited among lawns and trees on the far bank, and a series of shallow waterfalls. After that the coach continued on a relatively flat course, stopping for a few minutes outside Levens Hall, its famous topiary just visible over high stone walls. The gate pillars were topped by immense stone pineapples. Pink lupins and golden rod grew outside the farmhouse opposite, its windows lattice-paned and its roof mossy.

The landscape from here onwards was gentler than among the rugged mountains of the Lake District, trees arched overhead and black-faced sheep grazed on the lush green grass.

Morecambe Bay came into sight – the tide was out, exposing the vast Sahara-like expanse of golden but treacherous sands. At Milnthorpe there were houses with little flights of steps up to their doors (the lower level having once been used to house cattle) and arches built high for wagons to pass through. Then came Beetham with a river, pretty church and the Wheatsheaf Inn, to which I would return that night. We were at the Lancashire border, close to Leighton Hall (where eagles fly free), Carnforth, and Hest Bank of the golden sands where fishermen had left nets staked out to catch plaice or fluke and children were out shrimping.

Within minutes, we had reached Morecambe's lengthy promenade strung with fairy-lights, overlooking miles of sands, bathers and small sailing-boats at anchor. Morecambe runs into Lancaster which announces its presence only when one suddenly sees the parish church, castle, folly and high steeple of the Catholic church – all towering simultaneously above the urban skyline.

The coach crossed the bridge over the wide River Lune, there was a fleeting glimpse of the classical façades which give Lancaster its distinctive style, and then we halted in the coach station.

The Port That Used to Be

Lancaster's name describes its early origins – a Roman camp (*castra*) guarding the *Lune*. The river having been the lifeblood of the city until recently, it makes sense to go first to the old quay at the end of Damside Street, which is where the coaches stop.

St George's Quay, once humming with activity, is quiet now: silting prevents the big ships from coming upriver any longer as once they did to unload barrels and bales for the old warehouses that stand here, some with their wooden hoists still intact. The handsome Custom House, with sandstone portico and pillars, is closed.

The 18th century was the heyday of the port, hence the multitude of fine Georgian houses in Lancaster, built of creamy sandstone; and this quay would often have been piled high with mahogany from the West Indies, needed to make furniture for them (of which more later). The Lancaster merchants were involved in slave trading too. Now all is quiet, but in one preserved building I found The Smokehouse where one can buy (or order by post) delicacies smoked in the traditional way, over oak chips – Lune salmon, eel or quails – and potted Morecambe shrimps, venison, wild duck and much more.

A shady footpath called Vicarage Lane leads steeply up from the quay to the hill on which priory church and castle dominate the town. St Mary's, which stands on the site of a Norman monastery, is a mainly 15th-century building. Inside I found finely carved mediaeval choir stalls, now backed with panels of modern tapestry; battle-torn military banners hanging in one aisle; and red-and-white posies at the ends of the pews. Slate tombstones pave the floor. As at many bigger churches now, there is an adjoining café, in which the church's silver is on display. Standing outside, I looked down over the rooftops towards Morecambe Bay in one direction; in the other, there was a panorama of assorted belfries, cupola, clock-tower and the great Ashton monument on its hilltop towering over all. Tiny alleys zigzagged downhill among the houses.

Alongside the church is the Norman castle – built on this hilltop for the same reason as Roman fortifications earlier on, to defend the crossing over the Lune. The Elizabethan turret above the ancient keep was designed to hold a beacon at the time when a Spanish invasion was feared. For centuries the castle has housed a large prison (but parts are open to view – including some rather creepy dungeons and the adjoining Regency shire hall), and also a court where celebrated trials have been held – George Fox faced prosecution here for his Quaker preaching in the churchyard, witches were condemned to death, and more recently the whole area was cordoned off while the 'Mr Asia' drugs trial took place. The great John of Gaunt gatehouse, named after the famous second Duke of Lancaster, is still equipped with a portcullis: the gate was built by Henry V; later his statue was placed on it. To this day, it is the monarch who is Duke of Lancaster. Around the gateway are grouped Georgian houses with pretty fanlights, and cobble-stones in patterns. The stone bollards were hot from the blazing sunshine, and the smell of new-mown lawn scented the warm air.

A partly cobbled way descends to Church Street; passing (on Castle Hill) a cottage housing a small museum of social history, and the Judges' Lodgings (on an embankment at the head of the street). This Jacobean house, the oldest in Lancaster because Royalists

burnt so many others during the Civil Wars, no longer accommodates the visiting judges but contains a museum with an outstanding
collection of dolls, and another of the fine furniture designed by
Lancaster's celebrated cabinetmaker, Richard Gillow, in the 18th
century. Church Street and surrounding roads have Georgian
houses in the cellars of which Roman finds have been dug up.
Several are now antique shops or restaurants; one, where Bonnie
Prince Charlie stayed on his march south in 1745, is the Conserva-
tive Club – beside its fine doorway, I spotted the old iron snuffer in
which were dowsed the torches used at night before street lighting
came in.

I turned down little Sun Street to see the Music (or Muses)
Room, a gem of a building, the original purpose of which is a
mystery – it is such an elegant house to find in a cobbled byway.
Corinthian pilasters decorate its narrow three-storied façade; and
inside you can see remarkable plasterwork (the top floor can be
rented as a holiday flat from the Landmark Trust which carried out
the restoration of the building a few years ago).

A passage leads to Market Street, now pedestrianised for
shoppers and attractively laid out with paving, trees and bollards.
Here is the City Museum in a Georgian building (once the town
hall) that has scallop-shell decoration over its doorways and an
assortment of exhibits – Cromwell's iron money-chest, a regimental
museum, ship models, more Gillow furniture and clog-makers'
tools (you can still buy in the city traditional Lancashire clogs –
wood soles, laced leather uppers). There are quiz sheets to keep
children busy; and free guided walks start from here.

Little passageways (Bashful Alley and Old Sir Simon's
Arcade are two) lead off the street – some to the Market Hall, built
in the early years of Victoria's reign. Inside, it is spanned by a great
girdered roof rather like one of the more splendid Victorian rail
stations, where stalls sell local foods – Mr Burgess stocks the best
Lancashire cheese, white and crumbly.

A little further is Lancaster's pride – Dalton Square, late
Georgian – where flowerbeds and seats surround a particularly
striking statue of Queen Victoria with a parade of Victorian celebri-

ties around her feet, facing the grandiose Town Hall. (The Tourist Information Centre is in this square.)

It is not far to walk from here to Penny Street Bridge, over the Lancaster Canal, from which one can take a trip on the *Lancaster Packet*, a colourful narrowboat, with dinners served on board. There is a waterfront restaurant here, too. Or, more energetically, the canal can be walked – the towpath to the north goes through an area of old mills and other scenes of industrial archaeology, reaching Rennie Mackintosh's aqueduct (about 2 miles away) which carries the canal high over the river. The southward towpath is more rural, going past the village of Galgate (from which a bus can be taken back to Lancaster).

I had often seen from afar (it is impossible not to!) the colossal monument on a hill east of the city – a huge copper-domed memorial built by a local magnate (Lord Ashton) in memory of his wife. His wealth derived from manufacturing linoleum (the waterfront mill now produces vinyl) and in 1909 he spent what would now amount to millions of pounds on this incredible 'folly' tower, three stories of Corinthian pillars supporting a dome fit for a cathedral: the most sumptuous of useless buildings. A bus takes one to the gate of the surrounding park (previously quarries) but it is a stiff walk from there to the summit – worth it for the views, however. Shady paths twine among rocks and flowering shrubs and then one reaches the open sun-drenched summit, from which I could see the mountains of the Lake District westward across the blue sea of Morecambe Bay. Behind the monument is an orangery, and there is a little sunken garden with a pool. What a place from which to watch the sun set!

MORE PLACES TO VISIT include the following (the walks referred to are detailed in a booklet sold by the Tourist Information Centre): **Bolton-le-Sands** on Morecambe Bay. **Conder Green** country park with footpath along site of old railway. **Garstang** a route through the rolling countryside of The Fylde. **Glasson Dock** small, picturesque port. **Halton** walk back by riverside to Lancaster. **Hest Bank** for walks across the vast sands of Morecambe Bay, with guide. **Heysham** historic village with Norman remains; ferry to Isle of Man; nuclear power station being built – observation platform. **Hornsea Pottery** landscaped leisure park. Watch pottery being made and buy bargains. Rare breeds and children's farmyard. **Ingleton, Kirkby Lonsdale** along glorious Lune valley to attractive villages. **Leighton Hall**, Warton, the Gillows' Georgian mansion, ½ mile from bus stop. Displays of eagles flying. Gardens and woods. World's largest dolls' house. **Morecambe** long seafront. Largest ferris-wheel in the world. Aquarium and performing dolphins. Leisure park. Autumn illuminations. **Scorton** walk to Grizedale Reservoir. **Silverdale** walk through bird reserve, or through Eaves Wood to Arnside pele tower. **Steamtown**, Carnforth, Railway Museum. **Thurnham Hall** largely Elizabethan mansion. Replica of the Turin shroud. **University** Campus is open to public – lawns, pools, woodland, good bookshop, huge recreation centre, fish-and-chips. **Warton Crag** walk through wooded fells, views of bay.

For bus times, etc. tel. 0524 62004 or, for Ribble buses going further afield, 0524 64228. For other information, booklets, street plan, tel. the Tourist Information Centre, 0524 32878.

TO BRADFORD

Coaches depart from Lancaster daily in summer and the
journey takes about 3 hours. It goes through Yorkshire's hills
and dales: a very scenic ride. A good stop on the way would be
the historic town of Skipton, from which one can easily explore
the most beautiful of the Yorkshire dales.

We were quickly out of the city and following a winding road
dappled by sunlight through the overhead trees, with views of the
river snaking its way along the leafy valley. Stone farms, some
whitewashed, stood among the fields against a backdrop of faraway
blue hills, and then we passed a brickworks with great buckets
passing over the road on an aerial runway, to vanish over a hilltop.
The much-castellated castle at Hornby was built by one of the
knights who fought at Flodden. Cottages here have white doors with
black iron studs and decorative hinges. After crossing the river, we
climbed steadily up among the lovely hills – brown moors at the top,
drifts of conifers and very green grass on the foothills. Melling is
another pretty village with cottage gardens, and clematis rambling
over handsome porches. Sometimes there were madonna lilies
taller than the walls.

The road kept rising towards the jagged peaks on the horizon.
Burton-in-Lonsdale is a long village of stone houses and red roses
(even though Lancashire now lay behind us and we had entered
Yorkshire, county of the white rose).

Of Ingleton, one of the north's beauty spots (with waterfalls
and caves), we saw nothing as we paused only on the outskirts for a
20-minute refreshment break – at the smartest and cleanest café I
had yet encountered on any such break. The coach, which had been
full, left a number of young German backpackers here; and the
remaining passengers now divided equally between greyheads and
youngsters.

Onward once more, looking down on the world from a road
that ran straight and high, fringed with big daisies and harebells at

the foot of dry-stone walls. There were rocky outcrops in the green fields here, with saplings growing from any foothold they could find in the crags. We could see for miles, and not a town in sight. Beyond the top of the pass, we began to swoop downwards beside a forest of larch and ash. Down at Settle there was a river with weir, roses filling every garden, marigolds and nasturtiums in window-boxes, steep cobbled lanes and in the market square an arcaded hall. The only coach-travelling dog of all my journeys got on.

And still, all around, the panorama of green hills continued, or mountains blue and hazy in the noon sunshine. Blue cranesbill by the roadside was as brilliant as stained glass, cottage clematis purple as a bishop's stock. Peewits searched through stubble, and sweet peas had sown themselves in the wild.

We repeatedly crossed rivers and ran along roads shaded by sycamores or ash. At Gargrave (an attractive little place with Georgian houses, inns and interesting shops) there was a view of colourful narrowboats and launches downstream. Skipton was entered through handsome outskirts where parkland is the background, via some typical Yorkshire architecture – Victorian stone terraces. An old cornmill spans the river, with a great church and castle at the head of a very wide main street thronged with market stalls, flower baskets hanging from lamp-posts between the lime trees.

The coach stopped opposite the inconspicuous Unicorn Hotel among old warehouses, rippling roofs and canalside buildings. There were colourful narrowboats outside the lock on the canal. (How, I wondered, as the coach waited a few minutes, was the name 'Bold Venture Street' acquired by such a tiny, modest lane?)

We had almost seen the last of fine scenery by the time we got to Keighley – a town built with civic pride, when every building had its purpose clearly incised in the stone (public library, temperance institute, school board or the like), as if time would never alter the status quo; even the cycling club had had its name carved on a substantial building. But now industrial smells hang in the air, and Keighley takes more pride in boasting that it has its very own radio station and big leisure centre.

Rows of back-to-backs followed and then, after crossing the River Aire, we drove along its valley. The National Trust owns East Riddlesdon Hall (its tithe barn, lake and ducks visible from the coach) but most of the buildings along this road are suburban – though the wild hills are not far away, seen rising up from the other side of the valley. Bingley has its old mills with tall chimneys and a green surrounded by antique shops (the famous five-rise locks were not visible from the coach). I caught a fleeting glimpse of Saltaire, one of the very first (and most handsome) of garden cities laid out by mill-owner Titus Salt who named the township after himself. At Shipley we halted by the church, with an array of red- and yellow-canopied market stalls all around in a big modern square.

Within minutes we had reached Bradford, turning in through

the square where W. E. Forster's statue stands (the reformer who made free, universal education available for the first time). The great presses and huge rolls of newsprint of *The Bradford Argus* could be seen behind high plate-glass windows. We swung into the biggest and most modern of all the coach stations in England: a vast interchange where not only coaches and buses but rail and the city underground system all come together in one place, at the heart of one of Europe's greatest cities.

City of Wool

Bradford the golden! I stepped out of the high tech coach station, shiny and modern as an airport, into another era. Bradford was first among the industrial cities to scour a century's soot off its gloomy buildings – to reveal them as they were when first erected in newly quarried sandstone that glows like honey when the sun is on it.

The city reached its prime in Victoria's reign, with fortunes being made (or sometimes lost) from the weaving of worsted cloth. The textile barons, like all wealthy Victorians, travelled in Europe, bringing home works of art – and new ideas about architecture. No longer would they be satisfied with four walls and a roof in which to store their raw materials: the first street I walked down, Hall Ings (which described what it used to be – a hall by a meadow) is lined with wool warehouses each of which looks like an Italian palazzo. The Wool Exchange is straight out of Venice (except that the heads decorating its façade are those of Victorian wool merchants), the City Hall looks as if it has been transported by some colossal magic carpet from Florence.

Even after all this display of personal and civic pride, the wool merchants had more money than they could spend: many, there-fore, set up their own banks, and these too were built in resplendent style, pillars rising around carved doorways, domes above the pillars. I found it worth popping in and out just to look at the ceilings and other detail of the interiors. Even when a Penny Bank was established, to encourage workers to save, it was given the full architectural treatment (the Penny Bank, though it is now the great Yorkshire Bank, still has its name incorporated in the wrought-iron arch over the big doors). All these are within a short stroll north of the coach station.

I went inside the Wool Exchange, largely idle now that dealings are conducted by telephone or telex, and looked at the vast 'hammerbeam' roof – made not of oak but of iron girders, and with kings up there where angels would be if this were not a cathedral of trade. Sometimes antiques fairs or flea markets are held here. Tucked inconspicuously below the great hall is – typical of Bradford's eccentric quirks – a small perfumery. The shelves are lined with herbal extracts, aromatic oils and men's hair-lotions in the kind of old-fashioned bottles likely to have been found in the dressing-rooms of those bewhiskered merchants who once thronged the Exchange. Here the staff are sadly disappointed if you do *not* settle down to a long session of sniffing this and that before making your purchases; and for £7.50 you can have 50 ml of scent blended to your own preference, or to a very near match of the most expensive names in perfume.

Anyone may wander through the marble corridors of power in the City Hall, and often the Council chamber itself can be seen – circles of leather seats under a ceiling of plaster vines encircling stained-glass skylights. The walls are of figured mahogany and coloured marbles: the best that the world could produce was sent to Bradford. From its high tower, bells peal out a carillon, with carols at Christmas echoing over the city. But June is the time to be here, when the new Lord Mayor is installed – complete with Lord Mayor's Show progressing to the City Hall. (The Tourist Information Centre is here.)

The oldest pie-shop (of many) in Yorkshire is just across the way, and Philip Smith's reputation for excellence extends far beyond Bradford. In the window, the versatility of the pig is amply demonstrated in the piles of black puddings, cooked pig-cheeks and shanks straight out of the oven, among a dozen other local porcine delicacies.

A bus takes one out to Moorside and an old wool-spinning mill which has been restored as an industrial museum. (On the way, I passed the great Victorian cemetery, itself a showpiece vying with the famous one at Milan in the splendour of its sphinxes, obelisks and even more elaborate monuments; and opposite it the lovely lawns and flowers of Peel Park spread downhill.) The museum also houses old trams, steam engines, broughams and other vehicles. The greatest of the wool merchants were inventors as well as traders, and some of their engineering 'firsts' are shown in displays which start with prehistoric weaving and tell the story of wool over the centuries; often exhibits can be seen in motion.

I lingered over a small display about children in factories (some only 5 or 6 years old), and reformer Richard Oastler who campaigned to end this terrible abuse. Further on, there is the indenture of an apprentice, signed with a cross because he (like so many) was illiterate. Yet just such apprentices as these ultimately became superb master-craftsmen, creating the complex and beautiful machines of brass and steel now given an honoured place in the museum.

Bradford is still, but less exclusively, a textile city, though techniques have changed. At the museum shop, one can buy mementoes of the old days in the shape of wood bobbins, no longer used, converted into a variety of souvenirs.

Adjoining the mill is the manager's house. In the early days, owners lived beside their mills. But as they grew wealthier and their mills grew sootier, they moved out to country mansions and installed managers in their place. This house is just the way it used to be. The parlour has its horsehair sofa, aspidistra, Turkey carpet and albums of sepia photographs; the bathroom its loo patterned with blue flowers; the maidservant's room its iron bed. Even the museum café is in period, with Victorian light-fittings and tables on ornamental cast-iron legs.

Most of Bradford's textile mills have shops (accessible by bus) which are a bargain-hunter's paradise: as I write, I am wearing a top-quality lambswool cardigan sold for £1.90 because a button was missing. The Tourist Information Centre has a list of these mill-shops, indicating which sells men's suits, which knitting-wool and so on. At least one is within walking distance of the coach station. A favourite is Listers (in another Italianate building of great splendour) for the superb curtain velvets, normally £12–15 a metre, which sell at under £4. This is in the Manningham area where once-fine mansions of woolmen are now, in many cases, good small hotels.

Nearby is an extraordinary museum, with shop, containing a collection of gemstones and rocks that is in certain respects more comprehensive even than London's Geology Museum. Its bearded owner, George Hinchliffe, is especially proud of his display of dull-looking rocks which, under a type of ultra-violet lamp unique in this country, glow with fluorescent life in a dozen colours and patterns. All around are fossilised flowers, 'pudding stones', petrified palm trees and much else (even, rather oddly, a collection of walking-sticks that includes Chaplin's and Gladstone's). Many of these rocks, Mr Hinchliffe told me, he had amassed on round-the-world trips in 'old bangers' such as a Ford pick-up bought for £35 which he flogged over the Andes and across the Sahara.

I had underestimated Bradford and should have allowed myself more days there. There was no time left for me to walk round Little Germany (the quarter where Jewish refugees settled, prospered and built their fine mills and warehouses: several are now wine bars); the museums (films and photography in one; kaleidoscopic colour and the story of dyeing in another); the Art Gallery (which among other world-famous paintings has Gainsborough's 'Blue Boy' – Hockneys and Henry Moores too); the many beautiful parks (the Lister Park claims to be one of the best preserved examples of a traditional Victorian park, with every detail of the highest standard); Ponden Hall (which is the Thrushcross Grange of *Wuthering Heights* and where, in weavers' old cottages, one can see weavers at work); Bolling Hall (a Tudor mansion with ghosts); or the clog factory.

That is only the beginning of the list. I had sampled Yorkshire pudding in the hotel's carvery but not a Yorkshire high tea nor Yorkshire ale. What about Yorkshire brass-bands (Black Dyke Mills' or Hammond Sauce Works', for instance) or music-hall? There are several theatres in the city, and at St George's Hall the Hallé orchestra or rock concerts play to packed audiences. Of course, Bradford boasts outsize shopping centres, markets and sports centres. It also has Harry Ramsden's, where fish-and-chips has the status of haute cuisine; canal trips with dinner on board; and a choice from a hundred other good eating-places. Some visitors enjoy tours to see textiles being woven, or the *Bradford Argus* being printed; or even to look around the offices that handle their mortgage – Bradford is a great place for building societies' head-quarters and they, too, have their open-days, for Yorkshire ('Where there's muck, there's brass') is proud to show off its workaday life, particularly now that there's more money than muck around. Clearly, I would have to return again, perhaps on a 'heritage' weekend like the one I had so much enjoyed at Nottingham (see p. 83), but this time the theme would be either the Brontës, industrial archaeology or steam railways. Bradford, rightly labelling itself 'a surprising place', has so many different choices to offer.

MORE PLACES TO VISIT include: **Baildon** for walks on the moors, country park, beauty-spots. **Bingley** five-rise locks built in 18th century to lift boats up 60 feet. **Halifax** colonnaded Piece Hall: 18th-century wool market now filled with antique and craft shops; museum. **Ilkley** former spa town with historic buildings, some elegant shops. **Ilkley Moor** wild and craggy, fine views. **Keighley** steam train rides on scenic route to Haworth; Cliffe Castle; handloom weavers' homes; East Riddlesdon Hall – National Trust's Jacobean mansion. **Kildwick** riverside village with medi-aeval bridge, immensely long church, river walks. **Kirkstall Abbey** Norman ruins, museum, riverside park. **Leeds** another great wool city; shops in Victorian arcades; splendid art gallery. **Saltaire** see text. **St Ives** 800 acres with nature trail, lake, adventure playground etc. **Wharfedale** fells, crags, river views.

For bus timetables, route map, economy tickets, tel. 0274 720505. For other information, booklets, street plan, tel. Tourist Information Centre at the City Hall, 0274 729577.

In three hours, using the fast Rapide coach service again, I was home. At the beginning of the year I had never used a coach service before, but now I had completed some 3,000 miles of coach travel.

There was a lot of writing to be done. And then what? A real holiday was about due. I thumbed through the National Travel catalogue of British and European coach tours, and picked up a pen with which to fill in the booking-form – a convert to coaching.

APPENDICES

TOURIST BOARDS
British Tourist Authority, 64 St James's Street, London SW1. Tel. 01-629 9191. (This caters primarily for overseas visitors and covers the whole of Britian.)
English Tourist Board, 4 Grosvenor Gardens, London SW1. Tel. 01-730 3400.

REGIONAL TOURIST BOARDS
Cumbria 09662 4444
Northumbria 0632 817744
(Cleveland, Durham, Northumberland, Tyne & Wear)
North-West 0204 591511
(Cheshire, Lancashire, Merseyside and part of Derbyshire)
Yorkshire & Humberside 0904 707961
Heart of England 0905 29511
(Gloucester, Hereford & Worcester, Shropshire, Staffordshire, Warwickshire and West Midlands)
East Midlands 0522 31521
(Derbyshire, Leicestershire, Lincolnshire, Northamptonshire and Nottinghamshire)
Thames & Chilterns 0235 22711
(Oxfordshire, Berkshire, Bedfordshire, Buckinghamshire and Hertfordshire)
East Anglia 0473 214211
(Cambridgeshire, Essex, Norfolk and Suffolk)
London 01-730 0791
West Country 0392 76351
(Avon, Cornwall & Scilly Isles, Devon, part of Dorset, Somerset, Wiltshire)
Southern 0703 616027
(Hampshire, Isle of Wight, part of Dorset)
South East 0892 40766
(Sussex, Kent and Surrey)

WHERE I STAYED
Brighton Sillwood Lodge (0273 25493). A tiny Regency guest house with exceptional cooking. In a quiet courtyard near centre.
Bury St Edmunds (near) Popplebury (028483 660, or 01-373 0966). Artist's rural cottage, simple but attractively furnished; excellent wholesome food.
Canterbury Ebury Hotel (0227 68433). Victorian mansion on outskirts. Spacious rooms and big garden.
Cheltenham (near) Compton House*. Beautifully decorated country house with good food.
King's Lynn Stuart House Hotel (0553 2169). Good private hotel near the centre; quiet at weekends.
Lowestoft Spexhall Hall Farm, near Southwold*.
Nottingham See text.
Penzance Abbey Hotel (0726 66906). Exceptionally beautiful furnishings in an old house. Good English food.
Peterborough (near) Northborough Castle (0733 253 275). See text. I visited this, but did not stay overnight at Peterborough.
Plymouth (near) Overcombe Hotel, Yelverton (082285 3501). A well-run small hotel with moorland views, attractively furnished. Good cooking.
Portsmouth Tudor Court Hotel, Southsea (0705 20174). Small, well-run Victorian house near the centre yet quiet.
Salisbury (near) Stoke Farm, Broad Chalke*. Handsome house, attractively furnished, on a big farm. Good food.
Sherborne Milton Farm, near Shaftesbury*. Mediaeval house with antiques. Imaginative food.

Shrewsbury (near) Wrentnall House*. Elegant mansion, cordon bleu cookery.

Taunton (near) Old Manor Farmhouse, Norton Fitzwarren (0823 89801). Exfarm; a warm welcome, good food, real value for money.

Worcester (near) Pigeon House Farm (0886 32301). Old farmhouse, spacious rooms, good home cooking. Livestock includes rare breeds.

Northern Tour

Sheffield YMCA (0742 662267). See p. 169 and below.

Newcastle Eslington Villa, Gateshead (0632 876017). Victorian house in quiet setting, with ambitious menu.

Carlisle (near) Bessietown Farm (bookings: 04482 3902). Good home cooking and well furnished rooms in guest house on farm.

Lancaster Wheatsheaf Inn, near Milnthorpe (04482 2123). Typical country inn just off the main road.

Bradford Victoria Hotel (0274 28706). bargain weekends, see p. 206.

*At asterisked houses, bookings are made through Country Farm Holidays (tel. 0905 830899), an agency with a catalogue full of such places.

HOSTELS

Youth Hostels are open to people of all ages. Some have family bedrooms but most have only dormitories, male and female. As the buildings and amenities vary, hostels are graded; and there is a handbook describing each one. Prices per night for adults range from about £2 to over £3 (more in London hostels). Breakfasts cost about £1.20, evening 3-course meals (with tea) only a little more, and packed lunches about £1; or one may cook one's own food – ingredients are for sale. At the only hostel I have so far experienced (Truleigh Hill

near Brighton) the food was very good indeed. Another 65p or so is charged for the hire of a sleeping bag. To use Youth Hostels it is necessary to have a membership card (£5 for adults), obtainable from the YHA at 8 St Stephens Hill, St Albans, Herts. Nearly all hostels close between 10 a.m. and 5 p.m.; visitors are expected to give a hand with domestic chores – nothing onerous, though. Some hostels are modern; some in buildings of historic interest.

The hostels of the YMCA and YWCA are run differently. For a start (as my experience in Sheffield shows) you do not necessarily have to be young, a man, a Christian or a member of any association in order to book a YMCA room. The 80 hostels have a high proportion of single rooms – often with own basin, radio and perhaps w.c. or bath. Some double rooms are available too. There is a list of the hostels, showing what each provides (from cots to swimming pools, or rooms suitable for disabled people), and whether older and/or female visitors are acceptable. List obtainable from YMCA, 640 Forest Road, London E17 (01-520 5599).

YWCA hostels also, in many cases, take both men and women now. Some provide facilities for self-catering. Unlike hotels, they are most likely to have rooms free in the summer, when long-term residents go away. A list is obtainable from the YWCA at 2 Weymouth Street, London W1 (01-636 9722). Charges vary: at Sheffield, for example, I paid £6.50 for bed and breakfast.

OTHER SCENIC ROUTES

Coach services are constantly changing and new routes frequently start up. It is rather difficult to keep track of them all. I have listed below a few good routes, selected not just for their destinations but for the scenery along the way.

Newcastle–Alston–Penrith–Keswick (using the Hartside pass in the Pennines; at 1,800 feet, this is the highest coach route in England. Wrights, 0498 81200.

The Manchester coach heading for Glasgow (National Express service 805) passes spectacular parts of the Lake District.

The best of Northumbrian scenery lies north of Newcastle, seen from the National Express coach 374 heading for Edinburgh.

'Londonlink' routes – express services to Aldershot, Newbury, etc. From seven pick-up points in London, coaches go to towns surrounded by places of interest (historic, wildlife, Thames and country scenery). Alder Valley company, 0252 23322. Another fast and frequent service from London is the 190 'shuttle' to Oxford. Oxford South Midland Company, 0865 711312. Green Line coach routes out of London to sights in the surrounding countryside are detailed in a See the Sights brochure from the London Country Bus Co. (01-834 6563).

As a complete change from historic sights, Milton Keynes is worth a visit. The new express coach from Reading goes through lovely Chiltern scenery. United Counties, 0604 35661 or Alder Valley (see above).

The National Express coach from Blackpool to Norwich (service 952) goes through great Peak District scenery.

Service 356 (National Express) from Lincolnshire to East Anglia is a scenic ride.

CITY WEEKEND BREAKS
Here, together with the telephone numbers of their Tourist Information Centres, are some cities not already mentioned in this book which have bargain breaks in top hotels, with activities appropriate for visitors arriving without a car:

Bristol (0272 293891). Liverpool (051 709 3631), Manchester (061 247 3694), Stoke-on-Trent (0782 21242) and of course London (01-730 3450).

Information can also be had about breaks in these or other cities (with or without activities included) by obtaining the bargain weekend brochures of such big hotel chains or consortia as:
Best Western (01-940 9766), Comfort (01-221 2626), Crest (01-903 6422), Cunard (01-741 1555), Embassy (01-581 8222), Holiday Inn (01-794 7755), Ladbroke (01-734 6000), Rank (01-937 0088), Stardust Camelot (01-786 5500), Thistle (01-889 9336), Trusthouse Forte (01-567 3444).

EXPLORER TICKETS
In almost any part of the country, it is possible to use these economy tickets – which were first launched in 1981 in conjunction with my book *England by Bus*, proved a wildfire success, and have since increased in scope.

The tickets come in three types: the standard one; a family one for two adults and two children, a real bargain; and one for pensioners, at less than standard price. (The 1983 price for a standard Explorer ticket is £2.50.)

With such a ticket, you can travel all day long on the buses (except, in some areas, during the morning rush-hour). You can buy one or more Explorers in advance (at bus stations) to use later, when and where you like: the date of use has to be recorded on the ticket when you make your first trip of the day.

Because the tickets are intended for joy-riding, each town (or area) has its own Explorer leaflet, of the most interesting sights within a radius of maybe 10–20 miles. In some areas, presentation of the ticket at stately homes and suchlike entitles you to a discount on the admission fee.

COACH COMPANIES

The following is a list of operators running services throughout the year.

R. W. Appleby Ltd, Conisholme, Louth, Lincs. (tel. 050 785 361). Services from Humberside and Lincolnshire to London.

Blueline Coaches Ltd, 3/5 Spring Place, London NW5 (tel. 01-482 2402). Daily service Newcastle – South Shields – Sunderland – London (Kings Cross).

Flight Coach Travel Ltd, 284 Soho Road, Birmingham (tel. 021-523 4141). Service from Birmingham and the West Midlands to Heathrow Airport.

Go Whittle, Bridgnorth Road, Highley, Bridgnorth, Salop. (tel. 0746 861208). Services between Shropshire and London.

Grey-Green Coaches Ltd, 53/55 Stamford Hill, London N16 (tel. 01-800 8010). Services from London and Suburbs to most principal towns in East Anglia.

Jennings Coaches, Ashen, Sudbury, Suffolk (tel. 044 085 257). Ashen – Cavendish – Clare – Thaxted – Stansted Mountfitchet – Bishop's Stortford – Harlow – London (Kings Cross).

Norfolk Motor Services Ltd, Fullers Hill, Great Yarmouth, Norfolk (tel. 0493 4355). Services from most principal towns in East Anglia to London and Suburbs.

Premier Travel Services Ltd, Kilmaine Close, Kings Hedges Road, Cambridge (tel. 0223 69771). Services from principal East Anglian towns to many points in England.

Seamarks Coach & Travel Group Ltd, Dunstable Road, Luton, Beds. (tel. 0582 54191). Daily service London (Kings Cross) – Luton Airport.

Wallace Arnold Tours Ltd, 21 The Calls, Leeds, Yorks. (tel. 0532 36041). Services from Yorkshire and London to many destinations.

Whippet Coaches Ltd, Cambridge Road, Fenstanton, Huntingdon, Cambs. (tel. 0480 63792). Papworth Everard – St Ives – St Neots – Huntingdon – Biggleswade – Hatfield – London (Kings Cross).

Yelloway Motor Services Ltd, Weir Street, Rochdale, Lancs. (tel. 0706 47561). Services from North-West England to many destinations.

ACKNOWLEDGEMENTS

A collective thank-you to the staff of many tourist offices, guide agencies and bus stations at towns I visited, without whose sharing of local knowledge this book could not have been written; and particularly to Tony West and Alan Jessop of National Express whose advice and interest in the book were invaluable.